Common Core Mastery

Reading Informational Text

Grade **4**

Editorial Development: Teera Safi
Kira Freed
Lisa Vitarisi Mathews
Copy Editing: Anna Pelligra
Art Direction: Cheryl Puckett
Cover Design: Yuki Meyer
Cover Illustration: Chris Vallo
Illustration: Greg Harris
Design/Production: Marcia Smith
Jessica Onken

EMC 3204

Evan-Moor®
Helping Children Learn

Visit
teaching-standards.com
to view a correlation
of this book.
This is a free service.

Correlated to State and Common Core State Standards

Congratulations on your purchase of some of the finest teaching materials in the world.

Photocopying the pages in this book is permitted for <u>single-classroom use only</u>. Making photocopies for additional classes or schools is prohibited.

Contents

Introduction

Units

Science Articles

Geography Article

Social Studies Articles

Biography Articles

How-to Articles

What's in Every Unit?

Teacher resource pages are provided for lesson preparation and instructional guidance.

The Guided Reading Level helps identify appropriate texts.

Student objectives and content-area concepts are indicated.

A suggested learning path helps you pace the lesson.

Common Core State Standards correlations are located in each unit for easy reference.

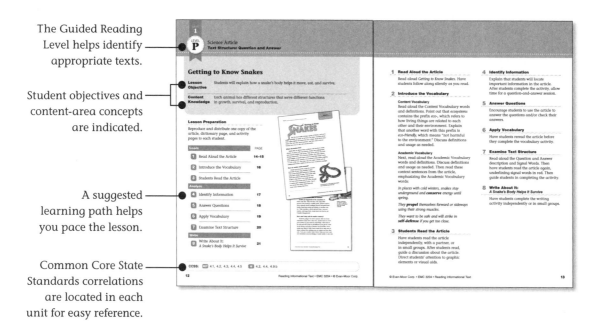

Content-area articles with embedded nonfiction text structures provide a variety of reading experiences.

Nonfiction Text Structures include:
- Question and Answer
- Cause and Effect
- Main Idea and Details
- Compare and Contrast
- Time Order

Labels indicate the content area.

Art and graphics provide additional information and context.

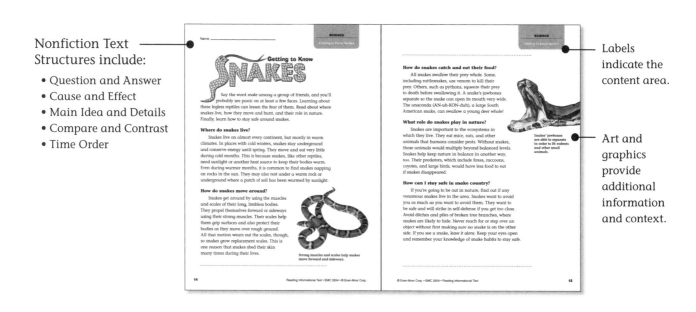

Student pages provide support for understanding the vocabulary, concepts, and structure of the text.

Dictionary

A dictionary page defines content and academic vocabulary words to help students better understand their use in the article.

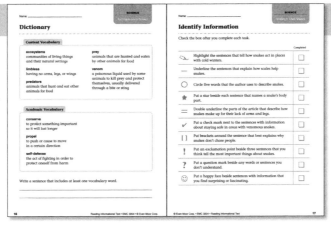

Identify Information

A close reading activity guides students to interact with the text and identify important information.

Answer Questions

A reading comprehension activity asks students to answer questions about the article, prompting them to examine it closely, and provides an informal assessment of students' understanding.

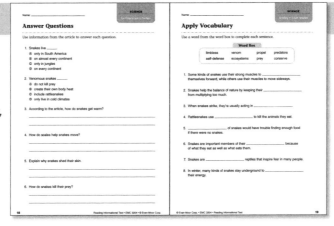

Apply Vocabulary

A vocabulary activity provides students another opportunity to interact with key words from the article and apply them in a different context.

Text Structure

A text structure activity asks students to examine how information in the article is organized.

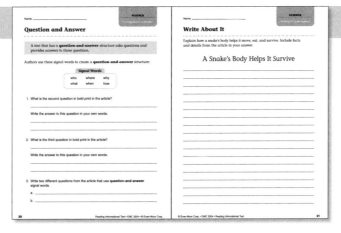

Write About It

The unit culminates with a text-based writing assignment.

Five Elements

A reproducible chart examines the five elements of informational texts, explains what each element is, and offers guiding questions to improve students' understanding of texts.

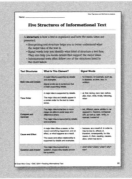

Five Structures

A reproducible chart describes how informational texts are organized and points out signal words associated with each text structure.

Correlations
Common Core State Standards

	Getting to Know Snakes	Weather and the Scientists Who Study It	From Power Plant to Light Bulb	The Mystery of the Matching Continents	Being an Active Citizen
RIT Reading Standards for Informational Text, Grade 4					
Key Ideas and Details					
4.1 Refer to details and examples in a text when explaining what the text says explicitly and when drawing inferences from the text.	●	●	●	●	●
4.2 Determine the main idea of a text and explain how it is supported by key details; summarize the text.	●	●	●	●	●
4.3 Explain events, procedures, ideas, or concepts in a historical, scientific, or technical text, including what happened and why, based on specific information in the text.	●	●	●	●	●
Craft and Structure					
4.4 Determine the meaning of general academic and domain-specific words or phrases in a text relevant to a grade 4 topic or subject area.	●	●	●	●	●
4.5 Describe the overall structure (e.g., chronology, comparison, cause/effect, problem/solution) of events, ideas, concepts, or information in a text or part of a text.	●	●	●	●	●
Integration of Knowledge and Ideas					
4.7 Interpret information presented visually, orally, or quantitatively (e.g., in charts, graphs, diagrams, timelines, animations, or interactive elements on webpages) and explain how the information contributes to an understanding of the text in which it appears.				●	●
W Writing Standards for Grade 4					
Text Types and Purposes					
4.2 Write informative/explanatory texts to examine a topic and convey ideas and information clearly.	●	●	●	●	●
Production and Distribution of Writing					
4.4 Produce clear and coherent writing in which the development and organization are appropriate to task, purpose, and audience.	●	●	●	●	●
Research to Build and Present Knowledge					
4.9.b Draw evidence from literary or informational texts to support analysis, reflection, and research. Apply grade 4 reading standards to informational texts.	●	●	●	●	●

Note: The header row spans the five units under a top heading "Units".

Units					RIT **Reading Standards for Informational Text, Grade 4**
How Countries Create Their Economies	Julia Morgan: Architect and Trailblazer	Roald Dahl: Master Storyteller	How to Keep Your Teeth and Gums Healthy	How to Make Snacks More Healthful	
					Key Ideas and Details
●	●	●	●	●	**4.1** Refer to details and examples in a text when explaining what the text says explicitly and when drawing inferences from the text.
●	●	●	●	●	**4.2** Determine the main idea of a text and explain how it is supported by key details; summarize the text.
●	●	●	●	●	**4.3** Explain events, procedures, ideas, or concepts in a historical, scientific, or technical text, including what happened and why, based on specific information in the text.
					Craft and Structure
●	●	●	●	●	**4.4** Determine the meaning of general academic and domain-specific words or phrases in a text relevant to a grade 4 topic or subject area.
●	●	●	●	●	**4.5** Describe the overall structure (e.g., chronology, comparison, cause/effect, problem/solution) of events, ideas, concepts, or information in a text or part of a text.
					Integration of Knowledge and Ideas
	●	●	●		**4.7** Interpret information presented visually, orally, or quantitatively (e.g., in charts, graphs, diagrams, timelines, animations, or interactive elements on webpages) and explain how the information contributes to an understanding of the text in which it appears.

Units					W **Writing Standards for Grade 4**
					Text Types and Purposes
●	●	●	●		**4.2** Write informative/explanatory texts to examine a topic and convey ideas and information clearly.
					Production and Distribution of Writing
●	●	●	●	●	**4.4** Produce clear and coherent writing in which the development and organization are appropriate to task, purpose, and audience.
					Research to Build and Present Knowledge
●	●	●	●	●	**4.9.b** Draw evidence from literary or informational texts to support analysis, reflection, and research. Apply grade 4 reading standards to informational texts.

Correlations
Texas Essential Knowledge and Skills

English Language Arts and Reading Standards for Informational Text, Grade 4	Getting to Know Snakes	Weather and the Scientists Who Study It	From Power Plant to Light Bulb	The Mystery of the Matching Continents	Being an Active Citizen	How Countries Create Their Economies	Julia Morgan: Architect and Trailblazer	Roald Dahl: Master Storyteller	How to Keep Your Teeth and Gums Healthy	How to Make Snacks More Healthful
110.15(b)(2) Reading/Vocabulary Development. Students understand new vocabulary and use it when reading and writing. Students are expected to:										
(A) determine the meaning of grade-level academic English words derived from Latin, Greek, or other linguistic roots and affixes	●	●	●	●	●	●	●	●	●	●
(B) use the context of the sentence to determine the meaning of unfamiliar words or multiple-meaning words	●	●	●	●	●	●	●	●	●	●
110.15(b)(11) Reading/Comprehension of Informational Text/Expository Text. Students analyze, make inferences, and draw conclusions about expository text and provide evidence from text to support their understanding. Students are expected to:										
(A) summarize the main idea and supporting details in text in ways that maintain meaning	●	●	●	●	●	●	●	●	●	●
(C) describe explicit and implicit relationships among ideas in texts organized by cause and effect, sequence, or comparison	●	●	●	●	●	●	●	●	●	●
(D) use multiple text features (e.g., guide words, topic and concluding sentences) to gain an overview of the contents of text and to locate information	●	●	●	●	●	●	●	●	●	●
110.15(b)(13) Reading/Comprehension of Informational Text/Procedural Texts. Students understand how to glean and use information in procedural texts and documents. Students are expected to:										
(A) determine the sequence of activities needed to carry out a procedure (e.g., following a recipe)		●	●	●	●	●			●	●
(B) explain factual information presented graphically (e.g., charts, diagrams, graphs, illustrations)		●	●	●	●	●				
110.15(b)(18) Writing/Expository and Procedural Texts. Students write expository and procedural or work-related texts to communicate ideas and information to specific audiences for specific purposes. Students are expected to:										
(A) create brief compositions that: (1) establish a central idea in a topic sentence; (2) include supporting sentences with simple facts, details, and explanations	●	●	●	●	●	●	●		●	●
(B) write letters whose language is tailored to the audience and purpose (e.g., a thank-you note to a friend) and that use appropriate conventions (e.g., date, salutation, closing)								●		
(C) write responses to literary or expository texts and provide evidence from the text to demonstrate understanding	●	●	●	●	●	●	●	●	●	●
110.15(b)(19) Writing/Persuasive Texts. Students write persuasive texts to influence the attitudes or actions of a specific audience on specific issues. Students are expected to write persuasive essays for appropriate audiences that establish a position and use supporting details.		●		●		●	●			

Reading Informational Text • EMC 3204 • © Evan-Moor Corp.

Overview of Articles and Writing Prompts

Title	Level	Content Area	Text Structure	Writing Prompt
How to Make Snacks More Healthful	O	Health	Compare and Contrast	Opinion/Persuasive
Getting to Know Snakes	P	Life Science	Question and Answer	Informative/Explanatory
Julia Morgan: Architect and Trailblazer	P	Biography (Arts)	Time Order	Argument
Being an Active Citizen	Q	Social Studies (Civics)	Main Idea and Details (Enumeration)	Informative/Explanatory
The Mystery of the Matching Continents	R	Geography	Cause and Effect	Argument
How to Keep Your Teeth and Gums Healthy	R	Health	Cause and Effect	Informative/Explanatory
Weather and the Scientists Who Study It	S	Earth Science	Main Idea and Details (Enumeration)	Argument
Roald Dahl: Master Storyteller	S	Biography (Arts)	Time Order	Informative/Explanatory
From Power Plant to Light Bulb	T	Physical Science	Time Order	Informative/Explanatory
How Countries Create Their Economies	T	Social Studies (Economics)	Compare and Contrast	Argument

Name: _____

Five Elements of Informational Text

An **element** can be thought of as an ingredient that exists in informational texts.

- Recognizing elements in a text helps you understand what it is about.
- Most nonfiction texts contain the elements listed in the chart below.
- Ask yourself guiding questions to identify what elements are in the informational texts you read.

Text Element	What Is This Element?	Guiding Questions
Purpose for Reading	This is your reason for reading the text. Sometimes you read: • to learn about a topic • for entertainment • to find specific facts about a topic	• Why am I reading this text? • What do I want to get out of the text? • Does the text match my purpose for reading? • Is the author's purpose to entertain, inform, argue, or teach?
Major Ideas	These are the most important messages in the text. They are key points that the author wants you to understand.	• What main ideas are being shared? • How are these ideas being presented?
Supporting Details	These are the details that help you understand the main idea(s) in the text.	• What are the supporting details for each major idea? • How are the supporting details presented?
Visuals and Graphics	These are pictures or graphics that help you understand what the text means. They include: • illustrations and photos • graphs, diagrams, and tables • charts and timelines	• What pictures or graphics does the author use to present information? • Do the pictures or graphics tell about major ideas or supporting details? • Do the pictures or graphics help me understand information from the text?
Vocabulary	These are words that you must understand in order to know what the text is about.	• What key words are used to tell about major ideas or supporting details? • Does the text contain any signal words that could have importance? • What words in the text appear bold or italicized?

Name: _____

Five Structures of Informational Text

A **structure** is how a text is organized and how the main ideas are presented.

- Recognizing text structure helps you to better understand what the major idea of the text is.
- Signal words help you identify what kind of structure a text has. They also help you locate details that support the major ideas.
- Informational texts often follow one of the structures listed in the chart below.

Text Structures	What Is This Element?	Signal Words
Main Idea and Details	A major idea is supported by details and examples. Signal words are in sentences that contain supporting details.	• for instance, for example, such as, to illustrate, another, also, in addition
Time Order	A major idea is supported by details. The major idea and details appear in a certain order for the text to make sense.	• at, first, during, next, last, before, after, then, while, finally, following, when
Compare and Contrast	The major idea is that two or more things are alike in some ways and different in others. The major idea is supported by details and examples.	• but, different, same, similar to, as opposed to, however, compared with, as well as, both, while, in contrast, instead of
Cause and Effect	A major idea offers a cause, or the reason something happened, and an effect, or what happens as a result. The cause-and-effect relationship is supported by details and examples.	• because, as a result of, in order to, may be due to, effects of, therefore, consequently, for this reason, if...then, causing, causes, allow, which has led to
Question and Answer	The major idea is posed as a question. Supporting details answer the question.	• who? what? where? when? why? how?

Science Article
Text Structure: Question and Answer

Getting to Know Snakes

Lesson Objective Students will explain how a snake's body helps it move, eat, and survive.

Content Knowledge Each animal has different structures that serve different functions in growth, survival, and reproduction.

Lesson Preparation

Reproduce and distribute one copy of the article, dictionary page, and activity pages to each student.

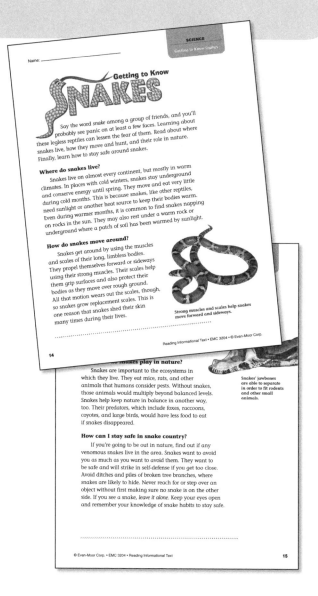

Name: _____

Getting to Know
SNAKES

Say the word *snake* among a group of friends, and you'll probably see panic on at least a few faces. Learning about these legless reptiles can lessen the fear of them. Read about where snakes live, how they move and hunt, and their role in nature. Finally, learn how to stay safe around snakes.

Where do snakes live?
Snakes live on almost every continent, but mostly in warm climates. In places with cold winters, snakes stay underground and conserve energy until spring. They move and eat very little during cold months. This is because snakes, like other reptiles, need sunlight or another heat source to keep their bodies warm. Even during warmer months, it is common to find snakes napping on rocks in the sun. They may also rest under a warm rock or underground where a patch of soil has been warmed by sunlight.

How do snakes move around?
Snakes get around by using the muscles and scales of their long, limbless bodies. They propel themselves forward or sideways using their strong muscles. Their scales help them grip surfaces and also protect their bodies as they move over rough ground. All that motion wears out the scales, though, so snakes grow replacement scales. This is one reason that snakes shed their skin many times during their lives.

Strong muscles and scales help snakes move forward and sideways.

Reading Informational Text • EMC 3204 • © Evan-Moor Corp.

14

... snakes play in nature?
Snakes are important to the ecosystems in which they live. They eat mice, rats, and other animals that humans consider pests. Without snakes, those animals would multiply beyond balanced levels. Snakes help keep nature in balance in another way, too. Their predators, which include foxes, raccoons, coyotes, and large birds, would have less food to eat if snakes disappeared.

Snakes' jawbones are able to separate in order to fit rodents and other small animals.

How can I stay safe in snake country?
If you're going to be out in nature, find out if any venomous snakes live in the area. Snakes want to avoid you as much as you want to avoid them. They want to be safe and will strike in self-defense if you get too close. Avoid ditches and piles of broken tree branches, where snakes are likely to hide. Never reach for or step over an object without first making sure no snake is on the other side. If you see a snake, *leave it alone*. Keep your eyes open and remember your knowledge of snake habits to stay safe.

© Evan-Moor Corp. • EMC 3204 • Reading Informational Text   15

CCSS: **RIT** 4.1, 4.2, 4.3, 4.4, 4.5   **W** 4.2, 4.4, 4.9.b

1 Read Aloud the Article

Read aloud *Getting to Know Snakes*. Have students follow along silently as you read.

2 Introduce the Vocabulary

Content Vocabulary

Read aloud the Content Vocabulary words and definitions. Point out that *ecosystems* contains the prefix *eco-*, which refers to how living things are related to each other and their environment. Explain that another word with this prefix is *eco-friendly*, which means "not harmful to the environment." Discuss definitions and usage as needed.

Academic Vocabulary

Next, read aloud the Academic Vocabulary words and definitions. Discuss definitions and usage as needed. Then read these context sentences from the article, emphasizing the Academic Vocabulary words:

*In places with cold winters, snakes stay underground and **conserve** energy until spring.*

*They **propel** themselves forward or sideways using their strong muscles.*

*They want to be safe and will strike in **self-defense** if you get too close.*

3 Students Read the Article

Have students read the article independently, with a partner, or in small groups. After students read, guide a discussion about the article. Direct students' attention to graphic elements or visual aids.

4 Identify Information

Explain that students will locate important information in the article. After students complete the activity, allow time for a question-and-answer session.

5 Answer Questions

Encourage students to use the article to answer the questions and/or check their answers.

6 Apply Vocabulary

Have students reread the article before they complete the vocabulary activity.

7 Examine Text Structure

Read aloud the Question and Answer description and Signal Words. Then have students read the article again, underlining signal words in red. Then guide students in completing the activity.

8 Write About It:
A Snake's Body Helps It Survive

Have students complete the writing activity independently or in small groups.

Name: _____

Getting to Know SNAKES

Say the word *snake* among a group of friends, and you'll probably see panic on at least a few faces. Learning about these legless reptiles can lessen the fear of them. Read about where snakes live, how they move and hunt, and their role in nature. Finally, learn how to stay safe around snakes.

Where do snakes live?

Snakes live on almost every continent, but mostly in warm climates. In places with cold winters, snakes stay underground and conserve energy until spring. They move and eat very little during cold months. This is because snakes, like other reptiles, need sunlight or another heat source to keep their bodies warm. Even during warmer months, it is common to find snakes napping on rocks in the sun. They may also rest under a warm rock or underground where a patch of soil has been warmed by sunlight.

How do snakes move around?

Snakes get around by using the muscles and scales of their long, limbless bodies. They propel themselves forward or sideways using their strong muscles. Their scales help them grip surfaces and also protect their bodies as they move over rough ground. All that motion wears out the scales, though, so snakes grow replacement scales. This is one reason that snakes shed their skin many times during their lives.

Strong muscles and scales help snakes move forward and sideways.

How do snakes catch and eat their food?

All snakes swallow their prey whole. Some, including rattlesnakes, use venom to kill their prey. Others, such as pythons, squeeze their prey to death before swallowing it. A snake's jawbones separate so the snake can open its mouth very wide. The anaconda (AN-uh-KON-duh), a large South American snake, can swallow a young deer whole!

What role do snakes play in nature?

Snakes are important to the ecosystems in which they live. They eat mice, rats, and other animals that humans consider pests. Without snakes, those animals would multiply beyond balanced levels. Snakes help keep nature in balance in another way, too. Their predators, which include foxes, raccoons, coyotes, and large birds, would have less food to eat if snakes disappeared.

Snakes' jawbones are able to separate in order to fit rodents and other small animals.

How can I stay safe in snake country?

If you're going to be out in nature, find out if any venomous snakes live in the area. Snakes want to avoid you as much as you want to avoid them. They want to be safe and will strike in self-defense if you get too close. Avoid ditches and piles of broken tree branches, where snakes are likely to hide. Never reach for or step over an object without first making sure no snake is on the other side. If you see a snake, *leave it alone.* Keep your eyes open and remember your knowledge of snake habits to stay safe.

Dictionary

Content Vocabulary

ecosystems
communities of living things
and their natural settings

limbless
having no arms, legs, or wings

predators
animals that hunt and eat other
animals for food

prey
animals that are hunted and eaten
by other animals for food

venom
a poisonous liquid used by some
animals to kill prey and protect
themselves, usually delivered
through a bite or sting

Academic Vocabulary

conserve
to protect something important
so it will last longer

propel
to push or cause to move
in a certain direction

self-defense
the act of fighting in order to
protect oneself from harm

Write a sentence that includes at least one vocabulary word.

_____

_____

Name: _____

Identify Information

Check the box after you complete each task.

		Completed
🖍	Highlight the sentences that tell how snakes act in places with cold winters.	☐
—	Underline the sentences that explain how scales help snakes.	☐
◯	Circle five words that the author uses to describe snakes.	☐
★	Put a star beside each sentence that names a snake's body part.	☐
=	Double underline the parts of the article that describe how snakes make up for their lack of arms and legs.	☐
✔	Put a check mark next to the sentences with information about staying safe in areas with venomous snakes.	☐
[ ]	Put brackets around the sentence that best explains why snakes don't chase people.	☐
!	Put an exclamation point beside three sentences that you think tell the most important things about snakes.	☐
?	Put a question mark beside any words or sentences you don't understand.	☐
☺	Put a happy face beside sentences with information that you find surprising or fascinating.	☐

Name: _____

Answer Questions

Use information from the article to answer each question.

1. Snakes live _____.
   - Ⓐ only in South America
   - Ⓑ on almost every continent
   - Ⓒ only in jungles
   - Ⓓ on every continent

2. Venomous snakes _____.
   - Ⓐ do not kill prey
   - Ⓑ create their own body heat
   - Ⓒ include rattlesnakes
   - Ⓓ only live in cold climates

3. According to the article, how do snakes get warm?

   _____

   _____

4. How do scales help snakes move?

   _____

   _____

5. Explain why snakes shed their skin.

   _____

   _____

6. How do snakes kill their prey?

   _____

   _____

Name: _____

Apply Vocabulary

Use a word from the word box to complete each sentence.

Word Box

| limbless | venom | propel | predators |
| self-defense | ecosystems | prey | conserve |

1. Some kinds of snakes use their strong muscles to _____ themselves forward, while others use their muscles to move sideways.

2. Snakes help the balance of nature by keeping their _____ from multiplying too much.

3. When snakes strike, they're usually acting in _____.

4. Rattlesnakes use _____ to kill the animals they eat.

5. _____ of snakes would have trouble finding enough food if there were no snakes.

6. Snakes are important members of their _____ because of what they eat as well as what eats them.

7. Snakes are _____ reptiles that inspire fear in many people.

8. In winter, many kinds of snakes stay underground to _____ their energy.

Question and Answer

A text that has a **question-and-answer** structure asks questions and provides answers to those questions.

Authors use these signal words to create a **question-and-answer** structure:

Signal Words

who	where	why
what	when	how

1. What is the second question in bold print in the article?

   _____

   Write the answer to this question in your own words.

   _____

   _____

2. What is the third question in bold print in the article?

   _____

   Write the answer to this question in your own words.

   _____

   _____

3. Write two different questions from the article that use **question-and-answer** signal words.

   a. _____

   b. _____

Name: _____

Write About It

....

Explain how a snake's body helps it move, eat, and survive. Include facts and details from the article in your answer.

A Snake's Body Helps It Survive

_____

_____

_____

_____

_____

_____

_____

_____

_____

_____

_____

_____

_____

_____

_____

_____

Weather and the Scientists Who Study It

Lesson Objective   Students will write an argument for why meteorologists need to use instruments to predict the weather.

Content Knowledge   Air pressure, wind speed, wind direction, precipitation, and special tools help people determine weather conditions in a particular time and place.

Lesson Preparation

Reproduce and distribute one copy of the article, dictionary page, and activity pages to each student.

<table>
<tr><td>Learn</td><td>PAGE</td></tr>
<tr><td>1 Read Aloud the Article</td><td>24–25</td></tr>
<tr><td>2 Introduce the Vocabulary</td><td>26</td></tr>
<tr><td>3 Students Read the Article</td><td></td></tr>
<tr><td>Analyze</td><td></td></tr>
<tr><td>4 Identify Information</td><td>27</td></tr>
<tr><td>5 Answer Questions</td><td>28</td></tr>
<tr><td>6 Apply Vocabulary</td><td>29</td></tr>
<tr><td>7 Examine Text Structure</td><td>30</td></tr>
<tr><td>Write</td><td></td></tr>
<tr><td>8 Write About It:
Do Meteorologists Need Instruments?</td><td>31</td></tr>
</table>

SCIENCE
Weather and the
Scientists Who Study It

Name: _____

WEATHER
and the Scientists Who Study It

Right this minute, many different types of weather are happening all around the world. Did you ever wonder what causes weather and how we know so much about it? We get weather information from scientists called *meteorologists*, who observe, study, and predict weather.

A thick band of air, called the *atmosphere*, surrounds our planet. It consists of layers of invisible gases. The atmosphere extends hundreds of miles into the sky. The lowest layer—the *troposphere*—is only about 6 to 9 miles (10 to 15 km) thick. The troposphere is where Earth's weather happens because this layer of air contains the most water. You usually can't see this water because it's in the form of an invisible gas called *water vapor*.

Many factors work together to create weather in the troposphere. The three main factors are sunlight, wind, and water. The sun heats up Earth's continents and oceans. Wind moves this heat around, and it also circulates the water vapor in the air.

The troposphere is the lowest layer in the atmosphere, where weather occurs.

thermosphere
mesosphere
stratosphere
troposphere

Reading Informational Text • EMC 3204 • © Evan-Moor Corp.

24

...ments.

- *Thermometers* measure the temperature of the air.
- *Anemometers* measure the speed of the wind.
- *Wind vanes* show from which direction the wind is blowing.
- *Rain gauges* measure rainfall.
- *Barometers* measure atmospheric pressure.

Meteorologists use computers to gather information. They get information from weather stations around the world, and they also study weather radar pictures that show rainfall. From space, weather satellites send information about clouds and temperatures.

Meteorologists study all this information. They use it to prepare weather charts and maps so they can predict what the weather will be in the future. The information helps them warn people so they can prepare for any severe weather that might be on its way.

The weather never stays the same for long in the troposphere. Throughout the year, it provides us with an endless variety of shows. Meteorologists around the world are always watching and studying those shows in an effort to better understand Earth's weather.

A meteorologist uses information from a computer to understand weather patterns.

© Evan-Moor Corp. • EMC 3204 • Reading Informational Text   25

CCSS: RIT 4.1, 4.2, 4.3, 4.4, 4.5   W 4.2, 4.4, 4.9.b

1 Read Aloud the Article

Read aloud *Weather and the Scientists Who Study It*. Have students follow along silently as you read.

2 Introduce the Vocabulary

Content Vocabulary

Read aloud the Content Vocabulary words and definitions. Point out the root word *sphere* in two of the words and review that a sphere is a round, 3-dimensional shape. Explain the meanings of the prefixes *atmo-* ("vapor") and *tropo-* ("turning" or "changing"). Discuss definitions and usage as needed.

Academic Vocabulary

Next, read aloud the Academic Vocabulary words and definitions. Discuss definitions and usage as needed. Then read the context sentences from the article, emphasizing the Academic Vocabulary words:

We get weather information from scientists called meteorologists, *who* **observe**, *study, and* **predict** *weather.*

They have weather stations that contain many types of **instruments**.

The information helps them warn people so they can prepare for any **severe** *weather that might be on its way.*

3 Students Read the Article

Have students read the article independently, with a partner, or in small groups. After students read, guide a discussion about the article. Direct students' attention to graphic elements or visual aids.

4 Identify Information

Explain that students will locate important information in the article. After students complete the activity, allow time for a question-and-answer session.

5 Answer Questions

Encourage students to use the article to answer the questions and/or check their answers.

6 Apply Vocabulary

Have students reread the article before they complete the vocabulary activity.

7 Examine Text Structure

Read aloud the Main Idea and Details description and Signal Words. Then have students read the article again, underlining signal words in red. Then guide students in completing the activity.

8 Write About It: *Do Meteorologists Need Instruments?*

Have students complete the writing activity independently or in small groups.

Name: _____

WEATHER
and the Scientists Who Study It

Right this minute, many different types of weather are happening all around the world. Did you ever wonder what causes weather and how we know so much about it? We get weather information from scientists called *meteorologists,* who observe, study, and predict weather.

A thick band of air, called the *atmosphere,* surrounds our planet. It consists of layers of invisible gases. The atmosphere extends hundreds of miles into the sky. The lowest layer—the *troposphere*—is only about 6 to 9 miles (10 to 15 km) thick. The troposphere is where Earth's weather happens because this layer of air contains the most water. You usually can't see this water because it's in the form of an invisible gas called *water vapor.*

Many factors work together to create weather in the troposphere. The three main factors are sunlight, wind, and water. The sun heats up Earth's continents and oceans. Wind moves this heat around, and it also circulates the water vapor in the air.

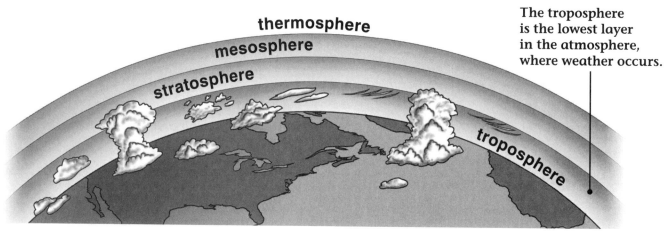

thermosphere

mesosphere

stratosphere

troposphere

The troposphere is the lowest layer in the atmosphere, where weather occurs.

The weather in the troposphere is constantly changing. For instance, water vapor in the air can cool and turn into rain clouds. Wind can later blow the clouds away, leaving clear blue skies. Dark clouds can scoot in, bringing a noisy thunderstorm.

Meteorologists study the effects of sunlight, wind, and water on the troposphere. In addition, they study changes in the weather.

Meteorologists get weather information from many sources. They have weather stations that contain many types of instruments.

- *Thermometers* measure the temperature of the air.

- *Anemometers* measure the speed of the wind.

- *Wind vanes* show from which direction the wind is blowing.

- *Rain gauges* measure rainfall.

- *Barometers* measure atmospheric pressure.

Meteorologists use computers to gather information. They get information from weather stations around the world, and they also study weather radar pictures that show rainfall. From space, weather satellites send information about clouds and temperatures.

A meteorologist uses information from a computer to understand weather patterns.

Meteorologists study all this information. They use it to prepare weather charts and maps so they can predict what the weather will be in the future. The information helps them warn people so they can prepare for any severe weather that might be on its way.

The weather never stays the same for long in the troposphere. Throughout the year, it provides us with an endless variety of shows. Meteorologists around the world are always watching and studying those shows in an effort to better understand Earth's weather.

Name: _____

Dictionary

Content Vocabulary

atmosphere
a layer of air surrounding a
planet or other body in space

temperature
a measure of the amount of
heat in something

troposphere
the lowest layer of Earth's
atmosphere; the layer in which
weather happens

water vapor
water in the form of an
invisible gas

Academic Vocabulary

observe
to watch and pay careful
attention to

predict
to say or estimate what will
happen in the future, often
after gathering information

instruments
tools, especially for taking or
recording measurements

severe
very intense, serious, or bad

Write a sentence that includes at least one vocabulary word.

_____

_____

Identify Information

Check the box after you complete each task.

		Completed
✎	Highlight the words and phrases that describe Earth's atmosphere.	☐
—	Underline the sentence that explains why water in the troposphere usually can't be seen.	☐
[ ]	Put brackets around the sentences that explain the main factors that create weather.	☐
◯	Circle the words that describe different types of weather.	☐
▲	Draw a triangle beside sentences that contain information about the role of wind in creating weather.	☐
~	Draw a squiggly line under any sentences that explain the main job of meteorologists.	☐
★	Put a star beside each instrument or other equipment used by meteorologists.	☐
✔	Put a check mark next to the sentence that explains what weather radar pictures show.	☐
☐	Draw a box around the sentence that explains why meteorologists warn people about severe weather.	☐
?	Put a question mark beside any words or sentences you don't understand.	☐

Name: _____

Answer Questions

Use information from the article to answer each question.

1. _____ is not one of the three main factors that create weather.
   Ⓐ Water
   Ⓑ Land
   Ⓒ Sunlight
   Ⓓ Wind

2. Meteorologists do not _____ weather.
   Ⓐ predict
   Ⓑ study
   Ⓒ cause
   Ⓓ observe

3. Why does Earth's weather happen in the troposphere?

   _____

   _____

4. What kind of weather would a meteorologist likely predict after seeing dark clouds?

   _____

   _____

5. Explain why weather stations are important.

   _____

   _____

6. What is the purpose of the weather charts and maps that meteorologists prepare?

   _____

   _____

Reading Informational Text • EMC 3204 • © Evan-Moor Corp.

Apply Vocabulary

Use a word from the word box to complete each sentence.

Word Box

troposphere	severe	water vapor	observe
temperature	predict	instruments	atmosphere

1. _____ turns into rain clouds when it gets cooler.

2. The layer of air in which weather happens is the _____.

3. People can prepare for _____ weather if they know ahead of time that it's coming.

4. Earth's _____ is a blanket of air that is hundreds of miles thick.

5. Anemometers are _____ that measure wind speed.

6. To measure the _____ of the air, a meteorologist uses a thermometer.

7. If you _____ dark clouds in the sky, a thunderstorm is likely to follow.

8. Meteorologists _____ that the weather will be sunny for the next three days.

Main Idea and Details

A text that has a **main idea and details** structure mentions the major ideas with supporting details in any order. The main idea is usually the topic sentence of a paragraph. Signal words indicate supporting details.

Authors use these signal words to create a **main idea and details** structure:

Signal Words

for instance	to illustrate	for example	in addition
another	such as	also	

1. The first paragraph tells us that _____ are the main topic of the selection.

2. What are two major ideas about the troposphere in the article?

   a. _____

   b. _____

3. Write two sentences from the article that use **main idea and details** signal words.

   a. _____

   _____

   _____

   b. _____

   _____

   _____

Name: _____

Write About It

· ·

Do meteorologists really need to use instruments in order to do their jobs?
Write an argument for why or why not. Include facts and details from the
article in your argument.

Do Meteorologists Need Instruments?

_____

_____

_____

_____

_____

_____

_____

_____

_____

_____

_____

_____

_____

_____

_____

Science Article
Text Structure: Time Order

From Power Plant to Light Bulb

Lesson Objective
Students will explain how electricity gets from power plants to people's homes.

Content Knowledge
Electrical energy travels in a closed path and can be converted to heat, light, and motion.

Lesson Preparation

Reproduce and distribute one copy of the article, dictionary page, and activity pages to each student.

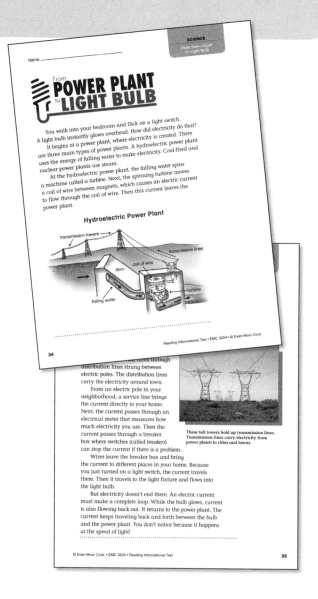

SCIENCE
From Power Plant to Light Bulb

Name: _____

From POWER PLANT to LIGHT BULB

You walk into your bedroom and flick on a light switch. A light bulb instantly glows overhead. How did electricity do that?

It begins at a power plant, where electricity is created. There are three main types of power plants. A hydroelectric power plant uses the energy of falling water to make electricity. Coal-fired and nuclear power plants use steam.

At the hydroelectric power plant, the falling water spins a machine called a *turbine*. Next, the spinning turbine moves a coil of wire between magnets, which causes an electric current to flow through the coil of wire. Then this current leaves the power plant.

Hydroelectric Power Plant

transmission towers
transmission lines
coil of wire
dam
turbine
falling water

Reading Informational Text • EMC 3204 • © Evan-Moor Corp.

34

...flows through distribution lines strung between electric poles. The distribution lines carry the electricity around town.

From an electric pole in your neighborhood, a service line brings the current directly to your home. Next, the current passes through an electrical meter that measures how much electricity you use. Then the current passes through a breaker box where switches (called *breakers*) can stop the current if there is a problem.

Wires leave the breaker box and bring the current to different places in your home. Because you just turned on a light switch, the current travels there. Then it travels to the light fixture and flows into the light bulb.

But electricity doesn't end there. An electric current must make a complete loop. While the bulb glows, current is also flowing back out. It returns to the power plant. The current keeps traveling back and forth between the bulb and the power plant. You don't notice because it happens at the speed of light!

These tall towers hold up transmission lines. Transmission lines carry electricity from power plants to cities and towns.

© Evan-Moor Corp. • EMC 3204 • Reading Informational Text

35

1 Read Aloud the Article

Read aloud *From Power Plant to Light Bulb*. Have students follow along silently as you read.

2 Introduce the Vocabulary

Content Vocabulary

Read aloud the Content Vocabulary words and definitions. Point out that the word *plant* in "power plant" is not referring to a living, growing thing. Rather, it refers to a building or structure. Point out that *transformer* is a multiple-meaning word. Ask students if they are familiar with the word *transformer*. Explain that some popular toys and videos are called by the same name. Discuss definitions and usage as needed.

Academic Vocabulary

Next, read aloud the Academic Vocabulary words and definitions. Discuss definitions and usage as needed. Then read these context sentences from the article, emphasizing the Academic Vocabulary words:

The current passes through a piece of equipment called a transformer, *which* **increases** *the current's power.*

When the transmission lines reach your town, the current passes through a substation, where a transformer **decreases** *the power.*

After that, the current flows through **distribution** *lines strung between electric poles.*

3 Students Read the Article

Have students read the article independently, with a partner, or in small groups. After students read, guide a discussion about the article. Direct students' attention to graphic elements or visual aids.

4 Identify Information

Explain that students will locate important information in the article. After students complete the activity, allow time for a question-and-answer session.

5 Answer Questions

Encourage students to use the article to answer the questions and/or check their answers.

6 Apply Vocabulary

Have students reread the article before they complete the vocabulary activity.

7 Examine Text Structure

Read aloud the Time Order description and Signal Words. Then have students read the article again, underlining signal words in red. Then guide students in completing the activity.

8 Write About It:
How We Get Electricity

Have students complete the writing activity independently or in small groups.

Name: _____

From POWER PLANT to LIGHT BULB

You walk into your bedroom and flick on a light switch. A light bulb instantly glows overhead. How did electricity do that?

It begins at a power plant, where electricity is created. There are three main types of power plants. A hydroelectric power plant uses the energy of falling water to make electricity. Coal-fired and nuclear power plants use steam.

At the hydroelectric power plant, the falling water spins a machine called a *turbine.* Next, the spinning turbine moves a coil of wire between magnets, which causes an electric current to flow through the coil of wire. Then this current leaves the power plant.

Hydroelectric Power Plant

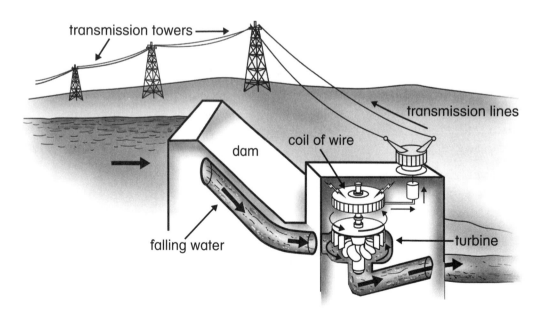

The current passes through a piece of equipment called a *transformer,* which increases the current's power. This high-powered current travels through transmission lines that stretch long distances. Tall metal towers hold them up.

When the transmission lines reach your town, the current passes through a substation, where a transformer decreases the power. After that, the current flows through distribution lines strung between electric poles. The distribution lines carry the electricity around town.

These tall towers hold up transmission lines. Transmission lines carry electricity from power plants to cities and towns.

From an electric pole in your neighborhood, a service line brings the current directly to your home. Next, the current passes through an electrical meter that measures how much electricity you use. Then the current passes through a breaker box where switches (called *breakers*) can stop the current if there is a problem.

Wires leave the breaker box and bring the current to different places in your home. Because you just turned on a light switch, the current travels there. Then it travels to the light fixture and flows into the light bulb.

But electricity doesn't end there. An electric current must make a complete loop. While the bulb glows, current is also flowing back out. It returns to the power plant. The current keeps traveling back and forth between the bulb and the power plant. You don't notice because it happens at the speed of light!

Name: _____

Dictionary

Content Vocabulary

breaker box
a box with switches that, in case of a problem, can stop an electric current from flowing to a place or piece of equipment

current
a flow of something, such as electricity or water, in a certain direction

electricity
a form of energy, carried through wires, that is needed to operate many lights, appliances, and machines

power plant
a building where a large amount of electricity is produced

transformer
a device that changes the power level of an electric current

turbine
a machine that spins as a result of moving air, water, or steam

Academic Vocabulary

increases
makes stronger, higher, larger, or greater in number

decreases
makes weaker, lower, smaller, or fewer in number

distribution
the act of delivering something to a place

Write a sentence that includes at least one vocabulary word.

_____

_____

Name: _____

Identify Information

Check the box after you complete each task.

		Completed
★	Put a star by each type of power plant mentioned.	☐
✔	Put a check mark beside each of the things a power plant may use to spin a turbine.	☐
✎	Highlight information that describes how electricity is created at a hydroelectric power plant.	☐
—	Underline the two ways in which a transformer changes an electric current's power.	☐
○	Circle different types of power lines through which electric current travels.	☐
[ ]	Put brackets around the name of the equipment that stops electric current in case of a problem.	☐
☐	Draw a box around the sentences that describe how a light bulb is able to glow after you turn on a light switch.	☐
∼	Draw a squiggly line under the sentence that tells exactly where electricity flows after it lights up a light bulb.	☐
!	Put an exclamation point beside the phrase that explains why you can't see electric current as it travels.	☐
?	Put a question mark beside any words or sentences you don't understand.	☐

Answer Questions

Use information from the article to answer each question.

1. _____ is <u>not</u> a type of power plant.
   - Ⓐ Nuclear
   - Ⓑ Coal-fired
   - Ⓒ Substation
   - Ⓓ Hydroelectric

2. According to the article, a spinning turbine _____.
   - Ⓐ increases the energy of falling water
   - Ⓑ moves a coil of wire between magnets
   - Ⓒ carries electricity to homes in your town
   - Ⓓ stops the flow of electricity if there is a problem

3. What materials listed in the article can power plants use to create electricity?

   _____

   _____

4. What is the purpose of transmission lines?

   _____

   _____

5. Explain the purpose of a breaker box.

   _____

   _____

6. According to the article, what is the complete loop made by an electric current?

   _____

   _____

Name: _____

Apply Vocabulary

Use a word from the word box to complete each sentence.

Word Box

power plant	transformer	increases
decreases	electricity	current
turbine	breaker box	distribution

1. Steam or falling water at a power plant makes a _____ spin.

2. The switches in a _____ stop electric current in case of a problem.

3. A _____ changes the power level of an electric current.

4. _____ powers a light bulb and causes it to glow.

5. When an electric current _____, it has more power than before.

6. After electricity leaves a substation, _____ lines carry it to your neighborhood.

7. At a substation, a transformer _____ power before electricity travels to your home.

8. A hydroelectric _____ uses the force of falling water to produce electricity.

9. Transmission lines carry a high-powered _____ of electricity.

Time Order

A text that has a **time order** structure presents the main idea and details in the order in which they happen.

Authors use these signal words to create a **time order** structure:

Signal Words

then	last	next	finally	when
first	before	after	following	while

1. What does the first paragraph in the article suggest about electricity? Why is it mentioned at that point in the article?

   _____

   _____

2. The third paragraph of the article tells us that before an electric current is created,

   _____

3. Write two sentences from the article that use **time order** signal words.

   a. _____

   _____

   b. _____

   _____

4. What is the final major idea mentioned in the article? Why is it mentioned last?

   _____

   _____

Name: _____

Write About It

Explain the path electricity takes from where it's created to your home.
Include descriptions of equipment and other details from the article.

How We Get Electricity

_____

_____

_____

_____

_____

_____

_____

_____

_____

_____

_____

_____

_____

_____

_____

_____

The Mystery of the Matching Continents

Lesson Objective   Students will write an argument for why Earth's continents and oceans may look different millions of years from now.

Content Knowledge   Processes such as erosion and earthquakes act on the earth and leave behind evidence of their occurrence in geographic features such as mountain ranges and coastlines.

Lesson Preparation

Reproduce and distribute one copy of the article, dictionary page, and activity pages to each student.

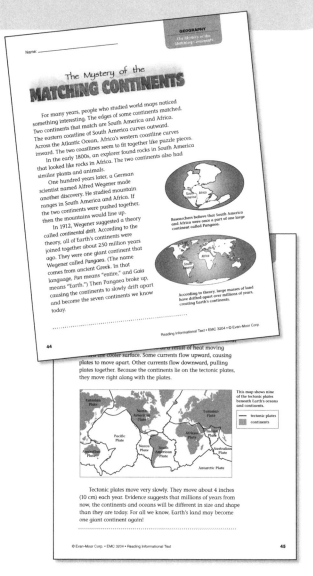

CCSS: **RIT** 4.1, 4.2, 4.3, 4.4, 4.5, 4.7   **W** 4.2, 4.4, 4.9.b

1 Read Aloud the Article

Read aloud *The Mystery of the Matching Continents*. Have students follow along silently as you read.

2 Introduce the Vocabulary

Content Vocabulary

Read aloud the Content Vocabulary words and definitions. Point out that *mantle* is a multiple-meaning word that can refer to one of Earth's layers or a loose cloak or cape. Discuss definitions and usage as needed.

Academic Vocabulary

Next, read aloud the Academic Vocabulary words and definitions. Discuss definitions and usage as needed. Then read these context sentences from the article, emphasizing the Academic Vocabulary words:

*The eastern **coastline** of South America curves outward.*

*In 1912, Wegener suggested a **theory** called continental drift.*

*They discovered that Earth's **surface** is made up of giant pieces of rock called tectonic plates.*

***Currents** form as a result of heat moving toward the cooler surface.*

***Evidence** suggests that millions of years from now, the continents and oceans will be different in size and shape than they are today.*

3 Students Read the Article

Have students read the article independently, with a partner, or in small groups. After students read, guide a discussion about the article. Direct students' attention to graphic elements or visual aids.

4 Identify Information

Explain that students will locate important information in the article. After students complete the activity, allow time for a question-and-answer session.

5 Answer Questions

Encourage students to use the article to answer the questions and/or check their answers.

6 Apply Vocabulary

Have students reread the article before they complete the vocabulary activity.

7 Examine Text Structure

Read aloud the Cause and Effect description and Signal Words. Then have students read the article again, underlining signal words in red. Then guide students in completing the activity.

8 Write About It:
Tectonic Plates Affect Earth's Surface

Have students complete the writing activity independently or in small groups.

The Mystery of the
MATCHING CONTINENTS

For many years, people who studied world maps noticed something interesting. The edges of some continents matched. Two continents that match are South America and Africa. The eastern coastline of South America curves outward. Across the Atlantic Ocean, Africa's western coastline curves inward. The two coastlines seem to fit together like puzzle pieces.

In the early 1800s, an explorer found rocks in South America that looked like rocks in Africa. The two continents also had similar plants and animals.

One hundred years later, a German scientist named Alfred Wegener made another discovery. He studied mountain ranges in South America and Africa. If the two continents were pushed together, then the mountains would line up.

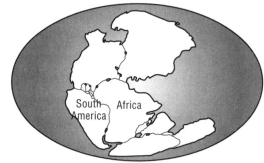

Researchers believe that South America and Africa were once a part of one large continent called Pangaea.

In 1912, Wegener suggested a theory called *continental drift*. According to the theory, all of Earth's continents were joined together about 250 million years ago. They were one giant continent that Wegener called *Pangaea*. (The name comes from ancient Greek. In that language, *Pan* means "entire," and *Gaia* means "Earth.") Then Pangaea broke up, causing the continents to slowly drift apart and become the seven continents we know today.

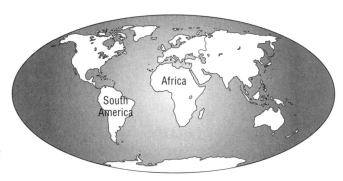

According to theory, large masses of land have drifted apart over millions of years, creating Earth's continents.

Many scientists didn't believe Wegener. They didn't understand how huge continents could move. But much later, in the 1960s, scientists developed a theory called *plate tectonics,* which explains how continents can move. They discovered that Earth's surface is made up of giant pieces of rock called *tectonic plates.* Some of these tectonic plates have continents on top of them, and others have oceans. These plates ride on hot, softer rock in the mantle—the layer underneath them. This hot, softer rock behaves like soft dough. It flows in currents because of heat deep inside Earth. Currents form as a result of heat moving toward the cooler surface. Some currents flow upward, causing plates to move apart. Other currents flow downward, pulling plates together. Because the continents lie on the tectonic plates, they move right along with the plates.

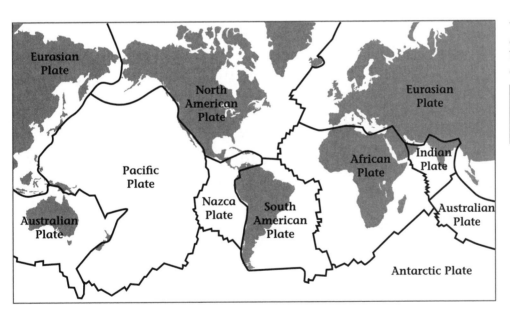

This map shows nine of the tectonic plates beneath Earth's oceans and continents.

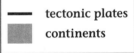

— tectonic plates

▨ continents

Tectonic plates move very slowly. They move about 4 inches (10 cm) each year. Evidence suggests that millions of years from now, the continents and oceans will be different in size and shape than they are today. For all we know, Earth's land may become one giant continent again!

Name: _____

Dictionary

Content Vocabulary

continental drift
the slow movement of Earth's
continents as tectonic plates shift

mantle
a thick layer of rock beneath
Earth's surface that, due to high
heat, moves very slowly

tectonic plates
huge sheets of rock that make up
Earth's surface

Academic Vocabulary

coastline
the boundary between land and
an ocean or lake

theory
an idea of how something works

surface
the outside or top of something;
the part of land or water that
touches the air above it

currents
streams of flowing air, matter, or
energy that move in a certain
direction

evidence
facts that show a theory or belief to
be true or false

Write a sentence that includes at least one vocabulary word.

_____

_____

Name: _____

Identify Information

Check the box after you complete each task.

		Completed
~	Draw a squiggly line under sentences that tell why people think South America and Africa were once joined.	☐
[ ]	Put brackets around time periods, lengths of time, and dates that are mentioned in the article.	☐
☐	Draw a box around the name of each continent the first time it appears.	☐
✎	Highlight the names of two theories discussed in the article.	☐
—	For each theory, underline one sentence that best explains what it is about.	☐
!	Put an exclamation point near any sentences that contain information about Earth's layers.	☐
○	Circle the sentences that describe rock in Earth's mantle and the ways it behaves.	☐
★	Put a star by the sentences that describe the speed at which tectonic plates move.	☐
✔	Put a check mark beside the sentence that tells what Earth's surface will probably be like millions of years from now.	☐
?	Put a question mark beside any words or sentences you don't understand.	☐

Answer Questions

Use information from the article to answer each question.

1. About 250 million years ago, _____.
   - Ⓐ there was no land on Earth
   - Ⓑ all of Earth's continents were joined together
   - Ⓒ Earth had many continents that were far apart
   - Ⓓ Earth's surface was covered in rock that behaved like soft dough

2. Alfred Wegener _____.
   - Ⓐ was an explorer
   - Ⓑ developed the theory of continental drift
   - Ⓒ said there was no such thing as Pangaea
   - Ⓓ was a Spanish scientist

3. Earth's surface is broken into giant pieces of rock called _____.
   - Ⓐ coastlines
   - Ⓑ currents
   - Ⓒ layers
   - Ⓓ tectonic plates

4. What did an explorer discover about the rocks, plants, and animals in South America and Africa?

   _____

   _____

5. What discovery was made about the coastlines of South America and Africa?

   _____

   _____

Name: _____

Apply Vocabulary

Use a word from the word box to complete each sentence.

Word Box

theory   surface   coastline   tectonic plates

mantle   currents   evidence   continental drift

1. Scientists have _____ that Earth's continents will be different in size and shape millions of years from now.

2. The unusual curves of the continent's _____ make it look like a huge puzzle piece.

3. Rock in the layer of Earth known as the _____ is hot and about as solid as soft dough.

4. According to the theory of _____, all of Earth's continents were once part of a single giant continent called *Pangaea.*

5. Alfred Wegener developed a _____ about how Earth looked millions of years ago.

6. Heat deep inside Earth moves toward the cooler _____.

7. Over millions of years, the movement of Earth's _____ can change how far away continents are from each other.

8. The flow of heat _____ causes tectonic plates to move together or apart.

Name: _____

Cause and Effect

A text that has a **cause-and-effect** structure includes a description of the cause and the resulting effects.

Authors use these signal words to create a **cause-and-effect** structure:

Signal Words

allow	if...then	in order to	as a result of
causing	effects of	consequently	may be due to
therefore	because	for this reason	which has led to

1. The article describes a series of cause-and-effect relationships. Write the answers on the lines to complete the cause-and-effect chain.

   Heat deep inside Earth causes rock to _____.

   Heat currents that flow downward cause plates to _____.

2. Write two sentences from the article that use **cause-and-effect** signal words.

   a. _____

   _____

   b. _____

   _____

3. What effect does the last paragraph suggest will happen many years from now?

   _____

   _____

Write About It

Suppose you are a scientist who believes that Earth's continents and oceans will be different millions of years from now. Write an argument for why you believe this. Include facts and details from the article.

Tectonic Plates Affect Earth's Surface

_____

_____

_____

_____

_____

_____

_____

_____

_____

_____

_____

_____

_____

_____

_____

Social Studies Article
Text Structure: Main Idea and Details

Being an Active Citizen

**Lesson
Objective** Students will explain what active citizenship is and how fourth graders can be active citizens.

**Content
Knowledge** Effective, informed citizenship is a duty of each citizen in the United States, demonstrated by voting and community service.

Lesson Preparation

Reproduce and distribute one copy of the article, dictionary page, and activity pages to each student.

Learn	PAGE
1 Read Aloud the Article	**54–55**
2 Introduce the Vocabulary	**56**
3 Students Read the Article	

Analyze	
4 Identify Information	**57**
5 Answer Questions	**58**
6 Apply Vocabulary	**59**
7 Examine Text Structure	**60**

Write	
8 Write About It: *Students Can Be Active Citizens*	**61**

CCSS: **RIT** 4.1, 4.2, 4.3, 4.4, 4.5, 4.7   **W** 4.2, 4.4, 4.9.b

1 Read Aloud the Article

Read aloud *Being an Active Citizen*. Have students follow along silently as you read.

2 Introduce the Vocabulary

Content Vocabulary

Read aloud the Content Vocabulary words and definitions. Point out that *issues* can be a noun or a verb. The definition for the noun is listed on the Dictionary page. As a verb, *issues* means "supplies or distributes" (as in a license or statement) or "flows from" (as in the smell of baked bread issuing from a kitchen). Discuss definitions and usage as needed.

Academic Vocabulary

Next, read aloud the Academic Vocabulary words and definitions. Discuss definitions and usage as needed. Then read these context sentences from the article, emphasizing the Academic Vocabulary words:

*This **historic** quote has **inspired** many people to take action and help their country as well as their **local** community.*

*After you learn about these issues, you may form **opinions** about them.*

3 Students Read the Article

Have students read the article independently, with a partner, or in small groups. After students read, guide a discussion about the article. Direct students' attention to graphic elements or visual aids.

4 Identify Information

Explain that students will locate important information in the article. After students complete the activity, allow time for a question-and-answer session.

5 Answer Questions

Encourage students to use the article to answer the questions and/or check their answers.

6 Apply Vocabulary

Have students reread the article before they complete the vocabulary activity.

7 Examine Text Structure

Read aloud the Main Idea and Details description and Signal Words. Then have students read the article again, underlining signal words in red. Then guide students in completing the activity.

8 Write About It:
Students Can Be Active Citizens

Have students complete the writing activity independently or in small groups.

Being an ACTIVE Citizen

Citizens can make a big difference in their community. In a country that is a democracy, citizens have a say in what happens, especially when they vote and perform community service. President John F. Kennedy once said, "Ask not what your country can do for you—ask what you can do for your country." This historic quote has inspired many people to take action and help their country as well as their local community. You do not have to be an adult to be an active citizen. You can start at any age.

President John F. Kennedy

One way to be an active citizen is to vote in elections. When you vote, you exercise your right to have a say in what happens. You must be eighteen or older to vote in a public election, but you can start voting in other elections even earlier. While adults vote for presidents, governors, mayors, and other officials, you can vote to elect leaders, too. You can vote to elect members of school government. Most teams and academic or social clubs have leadership positions that are chosen by a democratic vote. If you're not a member of a club or team, you can still learn more about voting by asking parents, teachers, and other adults how they make decisions in elections. In general, you'll want to make your vote count toward a purpose that you strongly believe in.

Voting is a right that every American citizen over the age of 18 is entitled to.

In order to vote wisely, it's important to learn about issues that affect your school or community. After you learn about these issues, you may form opinions about them. For example, imagine that you are voting for a class president at your school. Would you vote for a person whose speech is full of untrue information? Probably not, but you would need knowledge about the issues in order to tell if a speech was accurate or not. Similarly, would you vote for someone who doesn't care about any of the school's problems? No. You would probably vote for a student who seems enthusiastic about making things better for everyone at the school.

Your vote is important because it supports positive change in your community. You can be more successful in making changes if you are well informed.

Voting isn't the only way to be an active citizen. You can help to clean up your school or a neighborhood park, for example. You can hold a car wash to raise money for a new baseball field. You can volunteer your time at a library, a homeless shelter, a school, or another place that needs help. You can also be of service to an older adult by mowing his or her lawn.

Volunteering time to help your community is one way to be an active citizen.

Being an active citizen is an important part of living in a democracy. Active citizens stay well informed, vote, and volunteer. You are never too young to start being an active citizen.

Dictionary

Content Vocabulary

citizens
people who live in a community
or who belong by law to a country

democracy
a type of government that is run
by citizens who vote to choose
their leaders

elections
public votes to choose leaders

informed
having knowledge or education

issues
important topics that people are
thinking and talking about

Academic Vocabulary

historic
important in the past

inspired
filled people with a desire to take
action, often to do something
brave or creative

local
in or belonging to a certain city
or neighborhood

opinions
beliefs or views about something

Write a sentence that includes at least one vocabulary word.

_____

_____

Reading Informational Text • EMC 3204 • © Evan-Moor Corp.

Name: _____

Identify Information

Check the box after you complete each task.

	Task	Completed
◯	Circle an advantage of living in a democratic country.	☐
▱	Highlight the quotation in the article.	☐
—	Underline the sentence that mentions the public roles that adults can vote for in public elections.	☐
☐	Draw a box around the right that each person exercises by voting.	☐
[ ]	Put brackets around sentences that describe how you can vote before you turn eighteen.	☐
★	Put a star next to the sentence that tells why it is good to be well informed.	☐
=	Double underline the qualities of a student who would make a poor class president.	☐
~	Draw a squiggly line under each type of volunteer work mentioned in the article.	☐
✔	Put a check mark next to one thing you'd like to do to start being an active citizen.	☐
?	Put a question mark beside any words or sentences you don't understand.	☐

Answer Questions

Use information from the article to answer each question.

1. According to the article, one way to be an active citizen is to _____.

   Ⓐ do well in school

   Ⓑ discourage adults from voting

   Ⓒ learn about important local issues

   Ⓓ memorize historic quotes

2. To vote in a U.S. government election, a person must be _____ years of age.

   Ⓐ 16

   Ⓑ 18

   Ⓒ 20

   Ⓓ 21

3. The article does <u>not</u> mention _____ as a way to be an active citizen.

   Ⓐ voting

   Ⓑ volunteering

   Ⓒ cleaning up a park

   Ⓓ biking every day

4. What do you think President John F. Kennedy meant by the quote in the article?

   _____

   _____

5. What can you vote for, even if you're not yet eighteen years old?

   _____

   _____

Name: _____

Apply Vocabulary

Use a word from the word box to complete each sentence.

Word Box

local	historic	elections
issues	citizens	informed
inspired	opinions	democracy

1. An adult votes in many _____ during his or her lifetime.

2. People who live in a _____ have many opportunities to get involved and make a difference.

3. It's important to educate yourself about _____ before forming opinions about them.

4. During many difficult times in the past, a president's wise leadership has _____ people to work together to solve problems.

5. When you take time to become _____, you learn about important topics that affect your community.

6. Both young people and adults can be active _____.

7. Your _____ community can be your town or neighborhood.

8. An important past event, such as the first moon landing, is often described as _____.

9. People in the same family often have different _____.

Main Idea and Details

A text that has a **main idea and details** structure mentions the major ideas with supporting details in any order. The main idea is usually the topic sentence of a paragraph. Signal words indicate supporting details.

Authors use these signal words to create a **main idea and details** structure:

Signal Words

also	such as	for instance
another	to illustrate	for example

1. The main idea of the article is:

    _____

2. In the article, two major ideas about being an active citizen are:

    a. _____

    b. _____

3. Write two sentences from the article that use **main idea and details** signal words.

    a. _____

    _____

    b. _____

    _____

4. Would the article make sense to you if you read about voting and you did not live in a democracy? Why or why not?

    _____

    _____

Name: _____

Write About It

What is active citizenship? Explain how students in fourth grade can practice active citizenship. Use details from the article to support your answer.

Students Can Be Active Citizens

_____

_____

_____

_____

_____

_____

_____

_____

_____

_____

_____

_____

_____

_____

_____

_____

_____

How Countries Create Their Economies

Lesson Objective
Students will write an argument for how countries' decisions to import and export affect their economies.

Content Knowledge
All societies and nations must address the production, distribution, exchange, and consumption of goods and services.

Lesson Preparation

Reproduce and distribute one copy of the article, dictionary page, and activity pages to each student.

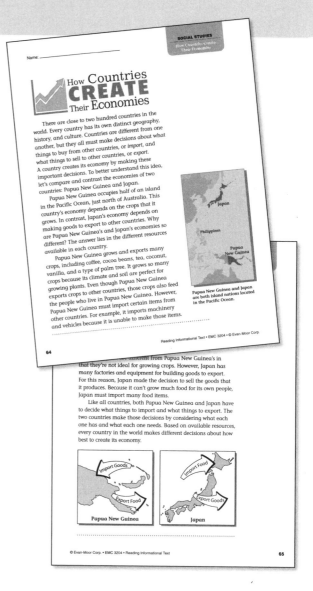

CCSS: RIT 4.1, 4.2, 4.3, 4.4, 4.5   W 4.2, 4.4, 4.9.b

1 Read Aloud the Article

Read aloud *How Countries Create Their Economies.* Have students follow along silently as you read.

2 Introduce the Vocabulary

Content Vocabulary
Read aloud the Content Vocabulary words and definitions. Point out that *import* and *export* both contain the root word *port,* which means "to carry." Explain that the prefix *im-* means "in," and the prefix *ex-* means "out." Discuss definitions and usage as needed.

Academic Vocabulary
Next, read aloud the Academic Vocabulary words and definitions. Discuss definitions and usage as needed. Then read these context sentences from the article, emphasizing the Academic Vocabulary words:

*Every country has its own **distinct** geography, history, and culture.*

*For example, it imports **machinery** and **vehicles** because it is unable to make those items.*

*Japan's climate and soil are different from Papua New Guinea's in that they're not **ideal** for growing crops.*

*For this reason, Japan made the decision to sell the goods that it **produces**.*

3 Students Read the Article

Have students read the article independently, with a partner, or in small groups. After students read, guide a discussion about the article. Direct students' attention to graphic elements or visual aids.

4 Identify Information

Explain that students will locate important information in the article. After students complete the activity, allow time for a question-and-answer session.

5 Answer Questions

Encourage students to use the article to answer the questions and/or check their answers.

6 Apply Vocabulary

Have students reread the article before they complete the vocabulary activity.

7 Examine Text Structure

Read aloud the Compare and Contrast description and Signal Words. Then have students read the article again, underlining signal words in red. Then guide students in completing the activity.

8 Write About It:
Countries Make Economic Decisions

Have students complete the writing activity independently or in small groups.

How Countries CREATE Their Economies

There are close to two hundred countries in the world. Every country has its own distinct geography, history, and culture. Countries are different from one another, but they all must make decisions about what things to buy from other countries, or *import*, and what things to sell to other countries, or *export*. A country creates its economy by making these important decisions. To better understand this idea, let's compare and contrast the economies of two countries: Papua New Guinea and Japan.

Papua New Guinea occupies half of an island in the Pacific Ocean, just north of Australia. This country's economy depends on the crops that it grows. In contrast, Japan's economy depends on making goods to export to other countries. Why are Papua New Guinea's and Japan's economies so different? The answer lies in the different resources available in each country.

Papua New Guinea grows and exports many crops, including coffee, cocoa beans, tea, coconut, vanilla, and a type of palm tree. It grows so many crops because its climate and soil are perfect for growing plants. Even though Papua New Guinea exports crops to other countries, those crops also feed the people who live in Papua New Guinea. However, Papua New Guinea must import certain items from other countries. For example, it imports machinery and vehicles because it is unable to make those items.

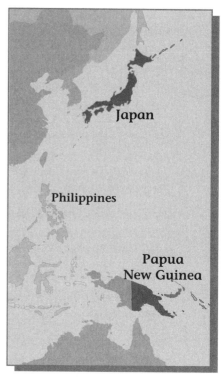

Papua New Guinea and Japan are both island nations located in the Pacific Ocean.

Now let's look at the economy of Japan, another island nation in the Pacific Ocean. Japan exports many valuable goods that are made by people and machines. These goods include plastics, metal machine parts, and cars. Japan is also known for making and exporting ships. Japan's

Japan exports cars and other valuable goods.

climate and soil are different from Papua New Guinea's in that they're not ideal for growing crops. However, Japan has many factories and equipment for building goods to export. For this reason, Japan made the decision to sell the goods that it produces. Because it can't grow much food for its own people, Japan must import many food items.

Like all countries, both Papua New Guinea and Japan have to decide what things to import and what things to export. The two countries make those decisions by considering what each one has and what each one needs. Based on available resources, every country in the world makes different decisions about how best to create its economy.

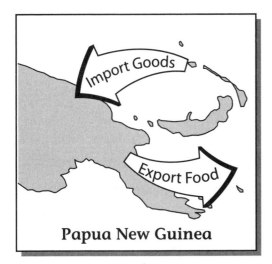

Papua New Guinea

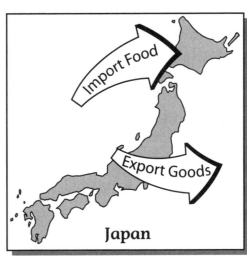

Japan

Dictionary

Content Vocabulary

economy
the way a country produces, sells, and buys needed goods and services

export
to sell goods and send them to another country or state

goods
things that are made or prepared so they can be sold

import
to buy goods and bring them in from another country or state

resources
supplies of things that are useful or valuable to people

Academic Vocabulary

distinct
different in ways that can be noticed

machinery
machines or machine parts

vehicles
machines, such as cars, used for transportation

ideal
exactly right for a certain purpose; perfect

produces
creates or causes

Write a sentence that includes at least one vocabulary word.

_____

_____

Identify Information

....

Check the box after you complete each task.

		Completed
🖍	Highlight the words in the first paragraph that describe the kinds of decisions that all countries must make.	☐
~	Draw a squiggly line under the valuable crops grown in Papua New Guinea.	☐
—	Underline the reason that Papua New Guinea grows so many crops.	☐
★	Put a star by the sentence that tells what Papua New Guinea does with its crops.	☐
=	Double underline the sentence that mentions what Papua New Guinea imports and why.	☐
[ ]	Put brackets around the sentences that tell about what Japan exports.	☐
◯	Circle the sentence that mentions Japan's climate and soil.	☐
✔	Put a check mark beside the sentence that explains how Japan gets food to feed its people.	☐
☐	Draw a box around any phrase in the last paragraph that explains how countries decide how best to create their economies.	☐
?	Put a question mark beside any words or sentences you don't understand.	☐

Answer Questions

Use information from the article to answer each question.

1. According to the article, _____ is <u>not</u> a major crop in Papua New Guinea.

   Ⓐ vanilla

   Ⓑ coconut

   Ⓒ cabbage

   Ⓓ coffee

2. _____ are <u>not</u> mentioned in the article as one of Japan's main exports.

   Ⓐ Bicycles

   Ⓑ Cars

   Ⓒ Ships

   Ⓓ Plastics

3. Why does Japan import so much food?

   _____

   _____

4. Why are the economies of Papua New Guinea and Japan so different?

   _____

   _____

5. When countries decide what to import and what to export, what two factors do they base their decisions on?

   _____

   _____

Name: _____

Apply Vocabulary

....

Use a word from the word box to complete each sentence.

Word Box				
ideal	import	economy	vehicles	produces
goods	export	resources	distinct	machinery

1. Coffee and tea are among Papua New Guinea's most useful

   _____.

2. A country decides what type of _____ to create after thinking about what it has and what it needs.

3. Plastics and ships are among the _____ that Japan makes to sell to other countries.

4. Countries that _____ cars make them in order to sell them.

5. Many kinds of metal _____ are required to make a car.

6. Cars, trucks, and buses are types of _____.

7. Every country, like every person, has a _____ history.

8. The _____ climate for growing apples is not too hot or cold.

9. When countries _____ food, they spend money to buy it from other countries.

10. Japan makes money by selling the cars that it _____.

Compare and Contrast

....

A text that has a **compare-and-contrast** structure compares, or describes similarities between things, and contrasts, or describes differences between things.

Authors use these signal words to create a **compare-and-contrast** structure:

Signal Words			
but	however	instead of	different from
both	same as	in contrast	compared with
while	similar to	as well as	as opposed to

1. The first paragraph explains that the selection will compare and contrast _____ and _____.

2. How are the two countries discussed in the article alike?

   _____

   _____

   _____

3. Write two sentences from the article that use **compare-and-contrast** signal words.

   a. _____

   _____

   _____

   b. _____

   _____

   _____

Name: _____

Write About It

....

Write an argument for why Papua New Guinea and Japan are making good choices for their economies. Include details about what Papua New Guinea and Japan choose to import and export.

Countries Make Economic Decisions

_____

_____

_____

_____

_____

_____

_____

_____

_____

_____

_____

_____

_____

_____

_____

_____

_____

Biography Article
Text Structure: Time Order

Julia Morgan: Architect and Trailblazer

Lesson Objective
Students will write an argument for why Julia Morgan's career achievements affected women in the field of architecture.

Content Knowledge
Important accomplishments of individuals and groups have contributed to modern social, political, economic, scientific, and technological practices and activities.

Lesson Preparation

Reproduce and distribute one copy of the article, dictionary page, and activity pages to each student.

BIOGRAPHY
Julia Morgan: Architect and Trailblazer

Name: _____

Julia Morgan: Architect and Trailblazer

Julia Morgan was born in 1872 in San Francisco, California. During her teens, she met an architect and became interested in designing buildings. Most girls in the 1800s did not go to college, but Julia was not like most girls. She attended the University of California, Berkeley, where she studied math and science. She earned a degree in civil engineering in 1894 and was the only female in her program.

After graduation, one of Julia's teachers urged her to attend a famous architecture school in France. She moved to France in 1896, even though the school did not allow women to attend. The next year, the school changed its rules and allowed women to apply. Julia became the school's first female student. She won medals for her work. After submitting an excellent design for a theater, she was awarded a certificate in architecture in 1902. She was the school's first female graduate.

Julia then returned to California and worked for an architect. She passed a test in 1904 and became California's first licensed female architect. She opened her own architecture office in San Francisco. Among her first projects were several buildings for a nearby women's college.

Mills College Library, in Oakland, California, was one of Julia Morgan's first projects.

74

Reading Informational Text • EMC 3204 • © Evan-Moor Corp.

...and other buildings after the earthquake.

Julia retired in 1951. During her lifetime, she designed over 700 buildings, most of them in California. One of her most famous buildings is Hearst Castle. Her projects included homes, schools, college buildings, churches, and museums. Julia's buildings are well made and beautiful. They never seem to go out of style.

Julia became a member of the California Hall of Fame in 2008. Her trailblazing career opened doors for women to enter the field of architecture.

The Bell Tower at Mills College was left standing after the 1906 earthquake.

Hearst Castle, in California, is one of Julia Morgan's most famous buildings.

© Evan-Moor Corp. • EMC 3204 • Reading Informational Text

75

CCSS: **RIT** 4.1, 4.2, 4.3, 4.4, 4.5, 4.7   **W** 4.2, 4.4, 4.9.b

1 Read Aloud the Article

Read aloud *Julia Morgan: Architect and Trailblazer.* Have students follow along silently as you read.

2 Introduce the Vocabulary

Content Vocabulary
Read aloud the Content Vocabulary words and definitions. Point out that the word *designing* is a form of the verb *design.* Explain that *design* is also used as a noun in the article. Discuss definitions and usage as needed.

Academic Vocabulary
Next, read aloud the Academic Vocabulary words and definitions. Discuss definitions and usage as needed. Then read these context sentences from the article, emphasizing the Academic Vocabulary words:

*After **submitting** an excellent design for a theater, she was awarded a certificate in architecture in 1902.*

*After that, she **gained** attention and new work, including the repair of a large hotel damaged in the earthquake.*

*Julia **retired** in 1951.*

*Her **trailblazing** career opened doors for women to enter the field of architecture.*

3 Students Read the Article

Have students read the article independently, with a partner, or in small groups. After students read, guide a discussion about the article. Direct students' attention to graphic elements or visual aids.

4 Identify Information

Explain that students will locate important information in the article. After students complete the activity, allow time for a question-and-answer session.

5 Answer Questions

Encourage students to use the article to answer the questions and/or check their answers.

6 Apply Vocabulary

Have students reread the article before they complete the vocabulary activity.

7 Examine Text Structure

Read aloud the Time Order description and Signal Words. Then have students read the article again, underlining signal words in red. Then guide students in completing the activity.

8 Write About It:
Julia Morgan's Influence

Have students complete the writing activity independently or in small groups.

Name: _____

Julia Morgan
Architect and Trailblazer

Julia Morgan was born in 1872 in San Francisco, California. During her teens, she met an architect and became interested in designing buildings. Most girls in the 1800s did not go to college, but Julia was not like most girls. She attended the University of California, Berkeley, where she studied math and science. She earned a degree in civil engineering in 1894 and was the only female in her program.

After graduation, one of Julia's teachers urged her to attend a famous architecture school in France. She moved to France in 1896, even though the school did not allow women to attend. The next year, the school changed its rules and allowed women to apply. Julia became the school's first female student. She won medals for her work. After submitting an excellent design for a theater, she was awarded a certificate in architecture in 1902. She was the school's first female graduate.

Julia then returned to California and worked for an architect. She passed a test in 1904 and became California's first licensed female architect. She opened her own architecture office in San Francisco. Among her first projects were several buildings for a nearby women's college.

Mills College Library, in Oakland, California, was one of Julia Morgan's first projects.

In 1906, there was a huge earthquake in San Francisco. Many buildings were destroyed, but a college bell tower designed by Julia was left standing. After that, she gained attention and new work, including the repair of a large hotel damaged in the earthquake. She designed hundreds of homes and other buildings after the earthquake.

The Bell Tower at Mills College was left standing after the 1906 earthquake.

Julia retired in 1951. During her lifetime, she designed over 700 buildings, most of them in California. One of her most famous buildings is Hearst Castle. Her projects included homes, schools, college buildings, churches, and museums. Julia's buildings are well made and beautiful. They never seem to go out of style.

Julia became a member of the California Hall of Fame in 2008. Her trailblazing career opened doors for women to enter the field of architecture.

Hearst Castle, in California, is one of Julia Morgan's most famous buildings.

Name: _____

Dictionary

Content Vocabulary

architect
a person who designs buildings
and makes sure they are built
correctly

certificate
a piece of paper proving that
something is true, especially that
a person has finished school or a
training program

civil engineering
the science of designing and
building bridges, roads, and
large buildings

designing
thinking about and planning
how to build or make something

licensed
having a legal paper giving
permission to do, use, or own
something

Academic Vocabulary

submitting
presenting to someone for
approval

gained
got or earned something

retired
stopped working, usually after
reaching a certain age

trailblazing
setting out in a new direction
and making it easier for others
to follow

Write a sentence that includes at least one vocabulary word.

_____

_____

Name: _____

Identify Information

....

Check the box after you complete each task.

		Completed
★	Put a star by the sentence that explains how Julia first became interested in architecture.	☐
◯	Circle the places where Julia went to school.	☐
🖊	Highlight each sentence that tells about Julia being the first woman to do something.	☐
☐	Draw a box around each year that Julia earned a degree, certificate, or license.	☐
[ ]	Put brackets around the type of building that was still standing after the 1906 San Francisco earthquake.	☐
✔	Put a check mark beside the sentence that tells when Julia retired.	☐
—	Underline the number of buildings Julia designed during her lifetime.	☐
~	Draw a squiggly line under the two sentences that best describe the qualities of Julia's buildings.	☐
!	Put an exclamation point next to the sentence that tells how Julia's work affected women.	☐
?	Put a question mark beside any words or sentences you don't understand.	☐

Name: _____

Answer Questions

Use information from the article to answer each question.

1. When Julia was a teenager, she became interested in _____.
   - Ⓐ moving to France
   - Ⓑ designing buildings
   - Ⓒ joining the California Hall of Fame
   - Ⓓ repairing buildings damaged by earthquakes

2. Julia's degree from the University of California, Berkeley, was in the field of _____.
   - Ⓐ medicine
   - Ⓑ architecture
   - Ⓒ museum studies
   - Ⓓ civil engineering

3. Julia went to France because _____.
   - Ⓐ she wanted to study architecture
   - Ⓑ her home in San Francisco was destroyed by an earthquake
   - Ⓒ her family wanted her to get married
   - Ⓓ she wanted to help women find meaningful work

4. How did the 1906 San Francisco earthquake help Julia's career?

   _____

   _____

5. Why does the article describe Julia's career as trailblazing?

   _____

   _____

   _____

Apply Vocabulary

....

Use a word from the word box to complete each sentence.

Word Box		
retired	certificate	gained
architect	trailblazing	licensed
designing	submitting	civil engineering

1. After _____ a school assignment, you will receive feedback and a grade from your teacher.

2. A _____ from a school proves that a person has completed a course of study.

3. Julia Morgan met an _____ who inspired her future career.

4. A person who does something that other people thought was impossible might be described as _____.

5. When Julia _____, she stopped designing buildings.

6. A _____ architect is permitted by law to work in the field of architecture.

7. If you want to build bridges, you should study _____ in college.

8. Julia studied architecture because she was interested in _____ buildings.

9. After the earthquake, Julia _____ new work.

Time Order

A text that has a **time order** structure presents the main idea and details in the order in which they happen.

Authors use these signal words to create a **time order** structure:

Signal Words

at	then	next	during	finally
first	last	after	before	following

1. The first paragraph of the article tells us that Julia Morgan

   _____ before becoming interested in architecture.

2. What happened a year after Julia moved to France?
   Why is this discussed after the information in the first paragraph?

   _____

   _____

3. Write two sentences from the article that use **time order** signal words.

   a. _____

   _____

   b. _____

   _____

Name: _____

Write About It

Write an argument for why Julia Morgan's career achievements affected women in the field of architecture. Include details from the article in your argument.

Julia Morgan's Influence

_____

_____

_____

_____

_____

_____

_____

_____

_____

_____

_____

_____

_____

_____

_____

_____

_____

_____

Roald Dahl: Master Storyteller

Lesson Objective
Students will explain who Roald Dahl was and what he did during his life.

Content Knowledge
Art, writings, music, and artifacts reflect culture.

Lesson Preparation

Reproduce and distribute one copy of the article, dictionary page, and activity pages to each student.

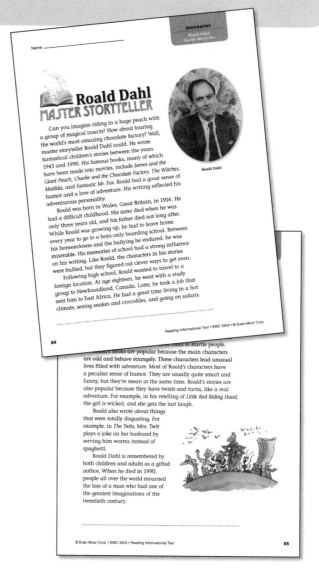

CCSS: **RIT** 4.1, 4.2, 4.3, 4.4, 4.5, 4.7   **W** 4.2, 4.4, 4.9.b

1 Read Aloud the Article

Read aloud *Roald Dahl: Master Storyteller.* Have students follow along silently as you read.

2 Introduce the Vocabulary

Content Vocabulary
Read aloud the Content Vocabulary words and definitions. Point out that *genre* is a borrowed word that comes from the French language and means "kind" or "sort." Discuss definitions and usage as needed.

Academic Vocabulary
Next, read aloud the Academic Vocabulary words and definitions. Discuss definitions and usage as needed. Then read these context sentences from the article, emphasizing the Academic Vocabulary words:

*Between his homesickness and the bullying he **endured**, he was miserable.*

*His memories of school had a strong **influence** on his writing.*

*Over the next several **decades**, Roald published other children's stories that were even more popular than the first one.*

*When he died in 1990, people all over the world **mourned** the loss of a man who had one of the greatest imaginations of the twentieth century.*

3 Students Read the Article

Have students read the article independently, with a partner, or in small groups. After students read, guide a discussion about the article. Direct students' attention to graphic elements or visual aids.

4 Identify Information

Explain that students will locate important information in the article. After students complete the activity, allow time for a question-and-answer session.

5 Answer Questions

Encourage students to use the article to answer the questions and/or check their answers.

6 Apply Vocabulary

Have students reread the article before they complete the vocabulary activity.

7 Examine Text Structure

Read aloud the Time Order description and Signal Words. Then have students read the article again, underlining signal words in red. Then guide students in completing the activity.

8 Write About It:
Roald Dahl's Life and Accomplishments

Have students complete the writing activity independently or in small groups.

Roald Dahl
MASTER STORYTELLER

Roald Dahl

Can you imagine riding in a huge peach with a group of magical insects? How about touring the world's most amazing chocolate factory? Well, master storyteller Roald Dahl could. He wrote fantastical children's stories between the years 1943 and 1990. His famous books, many of which have been made into movies, include *James and the Giant Peach, Charlie and the Chocolate Factory, The Witches, Matilda,* and *Fantastic Mr. Fox.* Roald had a great sense of humor and a love of adventure. His writing reflected his adventurous personality.

Roald was born in Wales, Great Britain, in 1916. He had a difficult childhood. His sister died when he was only three years old, and his father died not long after. While Roald was growing up, he had to leave home every year to go to a boys-only boarding school. Between his homesickness and the bullying he endured, he was miserable. His memories of school had a strong influence on his writing. Like Roald, the characters in his stories were bullied, but they figured out clever ways to get even.

Following high school, Roald wanted to travel to a foreign location. At age eighteen, he went with a study group to Newfoundland, Canada. Later, he took a job that sent him to East Africa. He had a great time living in a hot climate, seeing snakes and crocodiles, and going on safaris.

While Roald was working in Africa, World War II began. He joined the Royal Air Force, completed flight training, and flew many missions. After many adventures and several injuries, Roald moved to Washington, D.C., where he started to write short stories. His first children's book, *The Gremlins,* was published in 1943.

Over the next several decades, Roald published other children's stories that were even more popular than the first one. He also wrote stories for adults. Many of his adult stories were in the horror genre because he liked to startle people.

Roald's books are popular because the main characters are odd and behave strangely. These characters lead unusual lives filled with adventure. Most of Roald's characters have a peculiar sense of humor. They are usually quite smart and funny, but they're mean at the same time. Roald's stories are also popular because they have twists and turns, like a real adventure. For example, in his retelling of *Little Red Riding Hood,* the girl is wicked, and she gets the last laugh.

Roald also wrote about things that were totally disgusting. For example, in *The Twits,* Mrs. Twit plays a joke on her husband by serving him worms instead of spaghetti.

Roald Dahl is remembered by both children and adults as a gifted author. When he died in 1990, people all over the world mourned the loss of a man who had one of the greatest imaginations of the twentieth century.

Dictionary

Content Vocabulary

boarding school
a school where students live during the school year

fantastical
based on highly original and imaginative fantasy

genre
a specific category or type of writing, music, or art

retelling
a new version of a story

safaris
journeys to see or hunt wild animals, especially in East Africa

Academic Vocabulary

endured
lived through or put up with a difficult situation

influence
effect; the power to cause a change

decades
periods of ten years each

mourned
felt very sad, especially about a death or other loss

Write a sentence that includes at least one vocabulary word.

_____

_____

Name: _____

Identify Information

Check the box after you complete each task.

		Completed
[ ]	Put brackets around important dates in the article, including when Roald Dahl was born.	☐
	Highlight the names of books or stories written by Roald that are mentioned in the article.	☐
☐	Draw a box around each difficulty that Roald encountered as a child.	☐
★	Put a star by the lines that tell what Roald did in Africa.	☐
~	Draw a squiggly line under sentences that name other places where Roald lived.	☐
—	Underline the sentence that tells what Roald did when World War II started.	☐
◯	Circle the reason that Roald wrote horror stories for adults.	☐
✔	Put a check mark next to words and phrases that describe the characters in Roald's stories.	☐
!	Put an exclamation point next to sentences that describe why Roald Dahl's books are popular.	☐
?	Put a question mark beside any words or sentences you don't understand.	☐

Answer Questions

Use information from the article to answer each question.

1. Roald Dahl was born in _____.
   - Ⓐ East Africa
   - Ⓑ Great Britain
   - Ⓒ Canada
   - Ⓓ Washington, D.C.

2. Roald's children's books do <u>not</u> include _____.
   - Ⓐ *James and the Giant Peach*
   - Ⓑ *The Gremlins*
   - Ⓒ *Where the Wild Things Are*
   - Ⓓ *Charlie and the Chocolate Factory*

3. The best description of Roald Dahl is _____.
   - Ⓐ a struggling children's writer
   - Ⓑ a sad, lonely man
   - Ⓒ a very imaginative children's writer
   - Ⓓ a cruel, wicked man

4. What challenges did Roald face during his childhood?

   _____

   _____

5. How did Roald express his love of adventure in his books?

   _____

   _____

Name: _____

Apply Vocabulary

Use a word from the word box to complete each sentence.

Word Box

decades	genre	mourned
endured	safaris	boarding school
retelling	influence	fantastical

1. Fairy tale and science fiction are each a _____ of writing.

2. Roald Dahl _____ bullying as a child.

3. If you attend a _____, you sleep there instead of going home at night.

4. Roald's mother _____ the deaths of her husband and daughter.

5. Roald's adventurous personality had a strong _____ on his writing.

6. A _____ of a children's story might change the personalities of the characters.

7. If you go on _____ in East Africa, you're likely to see elephants, lions, and giraffes.

8. Roald wrote children's stories for more than four _____.

9. In one of Roald's _____ stories, a girl named Matilda uses her mind to move things.

Time Order

A text that has a **time order** structure presents the main idea and details in the order in which they happen.

Authors use these signal words to create a **time order** structure:

Signal Words

at	last	while	finally
next	first	later	following
when	after	before	

1. What did Roald Dahl endure in his life before finishing high school?

   _____

   _____

2. What is one important event that happened in Roald's life after he left East Africa?

   _____

3. Write two sentences from the article that use **time order** signal words.

   a. _____

   _____

   b. _____

   _____

4. What is the final major idea mentioned in the article? Why is it mentioned last?

   _____

   _____

Write About It

Write a letter to your teacher about Roald Dahl. Explain who he was and what he did during his life. Include details from the article in your letter.

Roald Dahl's Life and Accomplishments

_____

_____

_____

_____

_____

_____

_____

_____

_____

_____

_____

_____

_____

_____

_____

_____

_____

_____

_____

_____

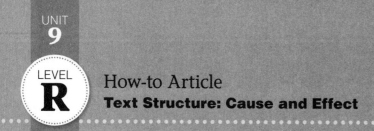

How to Keep Your Teeth and Gums Healthy

Lesson Objective   Students will explain what causes cavities in teeth and how to prevent them.

Content Knowledge   A decision-making process to select healthy practices leads to better overall health.

Lesson Preparation

Reproduce and distribute one copy of the article, dictionary page, and activity pages to each student.

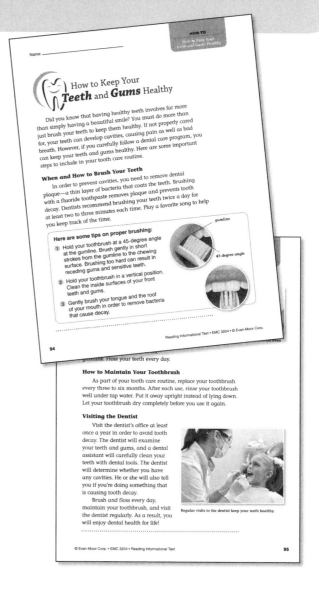

CCSS: RIT 4.1, 4.2, 4.3, 4.4, 4.5, 4.7   W 4.2, 4.4, 4.9.b

1 Read Aloud the Article

Read aloud *How to Keep Your Teeth and Gums Healthy*. Have students follow along silently as you read.

2 Introduce the Vocabulary

Content Vocabulary

Read aloud the Content Vocabulary words and definitions. Point out that the word *plaque* is a multiple-meaning word, or homonym. Provide students with the two definitions for the noun: *a sticky, often colorless film on teeth that is caused by and made up of bacteria* and *a flat, thin piece of metal or other material with words that honor a person or event*. Discuss definitions and usage as needed.

Academic Vocabulary

Next, read aloud the Academic Vocabulary words and definitions. Discuss definitions and usage as needed. Then read these context sentences from the article, emphasizing the Academic Vocabulary words:

Here are some important steps to include in your tooth care **routine**.

In order to **prevent** *cavities, you need to remove dental plaque—a thin layer of bacteria that coats the teeth.*

Brushing too hard can result in **receding** *gums and* **sensitive** *teeth.*

The dentist will **determine** *whether you have any cavities.*

3 Students Read the Article

Have students read the article independently, with a partner, or in small groups. After students read, guide a discussion about the article. Direct students' attention to graphic elements or visual aids.

4 Identify Information

Explain that students will locate important information in the article. After students complete the activity, allow time for a question-and-answer session.

5 Answer Questions

Encourage students to use the article to answer the questions and/or check their answers.

6 Apply Vocabulary

Have students reread the article before they complete the vocabulary activity.

7 Examine Text Structure

Read aloud the Cause and Effect description and Signal Words. Then have students read the article again, underlining signal words in red. Then guide students in completing the activity.

8 Write About It:
Causes and Prevention of Cavities

Have students complete the writing activity independently or in small groups.

Name: _____

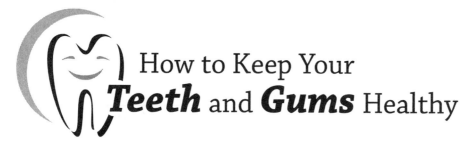

How to Keep Your *Teeth* and *Gums* Healthy

Did you know that having healthy teeth involves far more than simply having a beautiful smile? You must do more than just brush your teeth to keep them healthy. If not properly cared for, your teeth can develop cavities, causing pain as well as bad breath. However, if you carefully follow a dental care program, you can keep your teeth and gums healthy. Here are some important steps to include in your tooth care routine.

When and How to Brush Your Teeth

In order to prevent cavities, you need to remove dental plaque—a thin layer of bacteria that coats the teeth. Brushing with a fluoride toothpaste removes plaque and prevents tooth decay. Dentists recommend brushing your teeth twice a day for at least two to three minutes each time. Play a favorite song to help you keep track of the time.

Here are some tips on proper brushing:

1. Hold your toothbrush at a 45-degree angle at the gumline. Brush gently in short strokes from the gumline to the chewing surface. Brushing too hard can result in receding gums and sensitive teeth.

2. Hold your toothbrush in a vertical position. Clean the inside surfaces of your front teeth and gums.

3. Gently brush your tongue and the roof of your mouth in order to remove bacteria that cause decay.

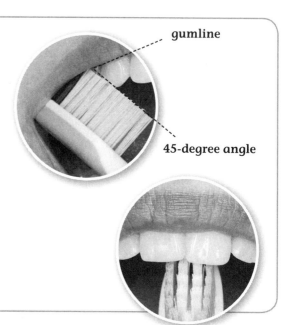

gumline

45-degree angle

When and How to Floss

Flossing clears out plaque and pieces of food stuck between your teeth that you missed when brushing. If plaque or food is left behind, then you may get a cavity. Wrap the floss tightly around one finger on each hand. Slide it up and down along each side of each tooth. Include the area just under the gumline. Floss your teeth every day.

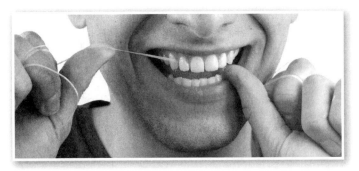

Wrap the floss around your fingers and slide it between your teeth.

How to Maintain Your Toothbrush

As part of your tooth care routine, replace your toothbrush every three to six months. After each use, rinse your toothbrush well under tap water. Put it away upright instead of lying down. Let your toothbrush dry completely before you use it again.

Visiting the Dentist

Visit the dentist's office at least once a year in order to avoid tooth decay. The dentist will examine your teeth and gums, and a dental assistant will carefully clean your teeth with dental tools. The dentist will determine whether you have any cavities. He or she will also tell you if you're doing something that is causing tooth decay.

Brush and floss every day, maintain your toothbrush, and visit the dentist regularly. As a result, you will enjoy dental health for life!

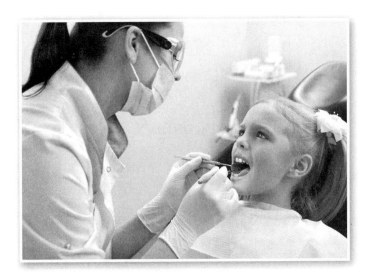

Regular visits to the dentist keep your teeth healthy.

Name: _____

Dictionary

Content Vocabulary

bacteria
small one-celled organisms that
can cause infections and disease

cavities
areas of teeth that are decayed

decay
the state or process of rotting

fluoride
a chemical often put in
toothpaste to help prevent
tooth decay

plaque
a sticky, often colorless film
on teeth that is caused by
and made up of bacteria

Academic Vocabulary

routine
a group of actions that are done
the same way every time

prevent
to stop something from
happening

receding
moving back or away

sensitive
quick to feel or respond to pain

determine
to reach a conclusion after
examining something carefully

Write a sentence that includes at least one vocabulary word.

_____

_____

Name: _____

Identify Information

Check the box after you complete each task.

		Completed
～	Draw a squiggly line under the sentence that tells what cavities cause.	☐
◣	Highlight the sentence that explains what dental plaque is.	☐
○	Circle the amount of time you should spend brushing your teeth.	☐
—	Underline sentences that tell how to move the toothbrush when you brush your teeth.	☐
✔	Put a check mark at the beginning of each sentence that explains how to floss your teeth.	☐
＝	Double underline the words that tell how often to floss your teeth.	☐
[ ]	Put brackets around the sentence that tells how often to replace your toothbrush.	☐
★	Put a star by each sentence that explains what to do with your toothbrush after you brush your teeth.	☐
!	Put an exclamation point beside each sentence that tells what happens when you visit the dentist.	☐
?	Put a question mark beside any words or sentences you don't understand.	☐

Name: _____

Answer Questions

Use information from the article to answer each question.

1. According to the article, dentists recommend brushing your teeth _____.
   Ⓐ once a day
   Ⓑ once a week
   Ⓒ twice a day
   Ⓓ twice a week

2. According to the article, flossing _____.
   Ⓐ kills bacteria that live on your teeth
   Ⓑ removes food from between your teeth
   Ⓒ heals cavities
   Ⓓ affects how your food tastes

3. According to the article, what can happen if you brush your teeth too hard?

   _____

   _____

4. What supplies do you need in order to take good care of your teeth at home?

   _____

   _____

5. What should you do to maintain your toothbrush?

   _____

   _____

6. What are the benefits of visiting a dentist regularly?

   _____

   _____

Name: _____

Apply Vocabulary

Use a word from the word box to complete each sentence.

Word Box

decay   plaque   receding   determine   prevent

routine   cavities   bacteria   sensitive   fluoride

1. Plaque is made up of tiny _____ that can cause infections.

2. If you brush too hard, your teeth may hurt or become _____.

3. Areas of tooth decay are called _____.

4. When gums are _____, they are pulling back from the base of the teeth.

5. Brushing and flossing can help _____ cavities.

6. When you floss, you remove food and _____ from between your teeth.

7. Toothpaste containing the chemical _____ helps keep teeth healthy and strong.

8. Brushing, flossing, maintaining your toothbrush, and visiting the dentist at least once a year all help to prevent tooth _____.

9. One job of a dentist is to _____ the cause of tooth decay.

10. Brushing my hair is part of my daily _____.

Cause and Effect

A text that has a **cause-and-effect** structure includes a description of the cause and the resulting effects.

Authors use these signal words to create a **cause-and-effect** structure:

Signal Words			
allow	therefore	consequently	because of
causing	effects of	for this reason	as a result
if…then	in order to	may be due to	

1. The article tells about the cause-and-effect relationship between

    _____ and cavities.

2. According to the article, what are the effects of flossing?

    _____

    _____

3. Write two sentences from the article that use **cause-and-effect** signal words.

    a. _____

    _____

    b. _____

    _____

4. According to the last paragraph, what will be the effect of following a program of tooth care?

    _____

    _____

Name: _____

Write About It

Explain what causes cavities in teeth and what you can do to prevent them. Use details from the article to support your answer.

Causes and Prevention of Cavities

_____

_____

_____

_____

_____

_____

_____

_____

_____

_____

_____

_____

_____

_____

_____

How-to Article
Text Structure: Compare and Contrast

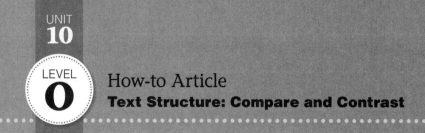

How to Make Snacks More Healthful

Lesson Objective
Students will write and support an opinion for whether or not people should substitute ingredients to make snacks more healthful.

Content Knowledge
A decision-making process to select nutritious foods and beverages leads to better overall health.

Lesson Preparation

Reproduce and distribute one copy of the article, dictionary page, and activity pages to each student.

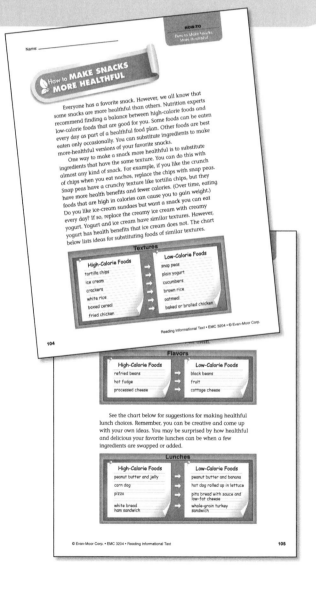

1 Read Aloud the Article

Read aloud *How to Make Snacks More Healthful.* Have students follow along silently as you read.

2 Introduce the Vocabulary

Content Vocabulary
Read aloud the Content Vocabulary words and definitions. Point out that most packaged food items have calories listed on the food label. Discuss definitions and usage as needed.

Academic Vocabulary
Next, read aloud the Academic Vocabulary words and definitions. Discuss definitions and usage as needed. Then read these context sentences from the article, emphasizing the Academic Vocabulary words:

*Nutrition **experts recommend** finding a balance between high-calorie foods and low-calorie foods that are good for you.*

*Other foods are best eaten only **occasionally.***

*You can **substitute** ingredients to make more-healthful versions of your favorite snacks.*

*For example, if you like the crunch of chips when you eat nachos, **replace** the chips with snap peas.*

*Snap peas have a crunchy texture like tortilla chips, but they have more health **benefits** and fewer calories.*

3 Students Read the Article

Have students read the article independently, with a partner, or in small groups. After students read, guide a discussion about the article. Direct students' attention to graphic elements or visual aids.

4 Identify Information

Explain that students will locate important information in the article. After students complete the activity, allow time for a question-and-answer session.

5 Answer Questions

Encourage students to use the article to answer the questions and/or check their answers.

6 Apply Vocabulary

Have students reread the article before they complete the vocabulary activity.

7 Examine Text Structure

Read aloud the Compare and Contrast description and Signal Words. Then have students read the article again, underlining signal words in red. Then guide students in completing the activity.

8 Write About It:
Substituting Ingredients to Make Foods Healthful

Have students complete the writing activity independently or in small groups.

How to **MAKE SNACKS MORE HEALTHFUL**

Everyone has a favorite snack. However, we all know that some snacks are more healthful than others. Nutrition experts recommend finding a balance between high-calorie foods and low-calorie foods that are good for you. Some foods can be eaten every day as part of a healthful food plan. Other foods are best eaten only occasionally. You can substitute ingredients to make more-healthful versions of your favorite snacks.

One way to make a snack more healthful is to substitute ingredients that have the same texture. You can do this with almost any kind of snack. For example, if you like the crunch of chips when you eat nachos, replace the chips with snap peas. Snap peas have a crunchy texture like tortilla chips, but they have more health benefits and fewer calories. (Over time, eating foods that are high in calories can cause you to gain weight.) Do you like ice-cream sundaes but want a snack you can eat every day? If so, replace the creamy ice cream with creamy yogurt. Yogurt and ice cream have similar textures. However, yogurt has health benefits that ice cream does not. The chart below lists ideas for substituting foods of similar textures.

Textures

High-Calorie Foods		Low-Calorie Foods
tortilla chips	→	snap peas
ice cream	→	plain yogurt
crackers	→	cucumbers
white rice	→	brown rice
boxed cereal	→	oatmeal
fried chicken	→	baked or broiled chicken

Another way to make a snack more healthful is to substitute ingredients that add flavor. Flavor, like texture, is another quality that we enjoy in our favorite foods. Instead of high-calorie foods, use low-calorie foods with similar flavors. For example, take a break from making nachos with large amounts of refried beans. Instead, try replacing the refried beans with black beans, salsa, or olives. For an ice-cream sundae, add fresh bananas and strawberries instead of hot fudge or caramel. Instead of using cheese from a spray can on your crackers, put cottage cheese on them.

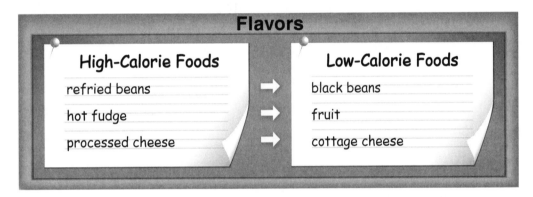

Flavors

High-Calorie Foods		Low-Calorie Foods
refried beans	➡	black beans
hot fudge	➡	fruit
processed cheese	➡	cottage cheese

See the chart below for suggestions for making healthful lunch choices. Remember, you can be creative and come up with your own ideas. You may be surprised by how healthful and delicious your favorite lunches can be when a few ingredients are swapped or added.

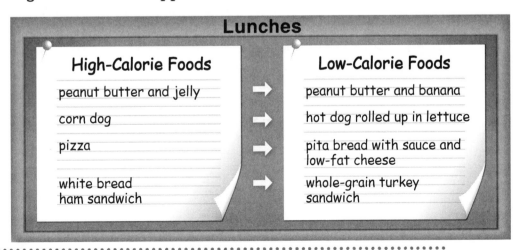

Lunches

High-Calorie Foods		Low-Calorie Foods
peanut butter and jelly	➡	peanut butter and banana
corn dog	➡	hot dog rolled up in lettuce
pizza	➡	pita bread with sauce and low-fat cheese
white bread ham sandwich	➡	whole-grain turkey sandwich

Name: _____

Dictionary

Content Vocabulary

calories
units of measure for the amount
of energy in food

flavor
taste

ingredients
food items that are used in
a recipe

nutrition
the study of eating the right
kinds of foods in order to grow
and be healthy

texture
the way something feels when
touched

Academic Vocabulary

experts
people who have special
knowledge of or skills in
a certain subject

recommend
to make a suggestion

occasionally
once in a while; not often

substitute
to use one thing instead of
another

replace
to use something to take the
place of another thing

benefits
good or helpful results

Write a sentence that includes at least one vocabulary word.

_____

_____

Identify Information

Check the box after you complete each task.

		Completed
—	Underline the sentence that tells what nutrition experts recommend.	☐
☐	Draw a box around the main idea about more-healthful snacks in the second paragraph.	☐
✎	Highlight each type of healthful food item listed in the article.	☐
[ ]	Put brackets around the sentence that explains what can happen over time as a result of eating foods that are high in calories.	☐
=	Double underline the phrases that explain what snap peas offer that tortilla chips do not.	☐
○	Circle the word (which appears twice) that tells how ice cream and yogurt are alike.	☐
!	Put an exclamation point beside healthful ingredients for nachos.	☐
★	Put a star beside the ice-cream toppings that you can use to make a sundae more healthful.	☐
✔	Put a check mark beside a healthful lunch alternative to pizza.	☐
?	Put a question mark beside any words or sentences you don't understand.	☐

Name: _____

Answer Questions

Use information from the article to answer each question.

1. According to the article, you should eat healthful foods _____.
   - Ⓐ only to lose weight
   - Ⓑ every day
   - Ⓒ occasionally
   - Ⓓ once a week

2. According to the article, foods you should eat only occasionally include _____.
   - Ⓐ cucumbers
   - Ⓑ bananas
   - Ⓒ caramel
   - Ⓓ sunflower seeds

3. Which food is healthful enough to eat every day?
   - Ⓐ hot fudge
   - Ⓑ cheese from a spray can
   - Ⓒ refried beans
   - Ⓓ broiled chicken

4. List ten healthful foods that are mentioned in the article.

   _____

   _____

   _____

5. What does the article suggest in the last paragraph?

   _____

   _____

Name: _____

Apply Vocabulary

Use a word from the word box to complete each sentence.

Word Box

nutrition	calories	occasionally	flavor
texture	benefits	recommend	substitute
experts	replace	ingredients	

1. Lettuce and tomatoes are common _____ in salads.

2. Over time, foods that are higher in _____ can cause people to gain weight.

3. The _____ of lettuce might be described as crispy.

4. A healthful _____ for crackers is cucumber slices.

5. When a food tastes good to you, it has a _____ you enjoy.

6. If you _____ cheese with salsa, your meal will be more healthful.

7. It's best to eat unhealthful foods only _____.

8. People who study the science of _____ understand which foods help people to be healthy.

9. Experts _____ eating healthful foods every day.

10. Foods that are good for you have health _____.

11. Nutrition _____ study the health benefits of various types of foods.

Name: _____

Compare and Contrast

A text that has a **compare-and-contrast** structure compares, or describes similarities between things, and contrasts, or describes differences between things.

Authors use these signal words to create a **compare-and-contrast** structure:

Signal Words			
but	as opposed to	compared with	however
instead of	as well as	same as	while
both	similar	different from	in contrast

1. The article compares and contrasts _____
   and _____.

2. How are tortilla chips and snap peas alike? How are they different?

   _____

   _____

   _____

3. Write two sentences from the article that use **compare-and-contrast** signal words.

   a. _____

   _____

   b. _____

   _____

Reading Informational Text • EMC 3204 • © Evan-Moor Corp.

Name: _____

Write About It

....

Do you think substituting ingredients to make snacks more healthful is
a good idea? Why or why not? Include details from the article in your answer.

Substituting Ingredients
to Make Foods Healthful

_____

_____

_____

_____

_____

_____

_____

_____

_____

_____

_____

_____

_____

_____

_____

Answer Key

Unit 1

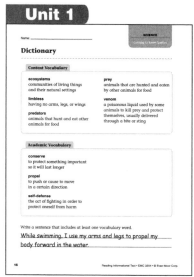

TE Page 16 / SB Page 8

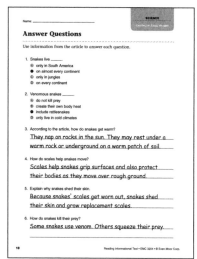

TE Page 18 / SB Page 10

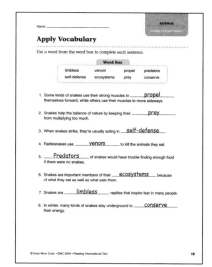

TE Page 19 / SB Page 11

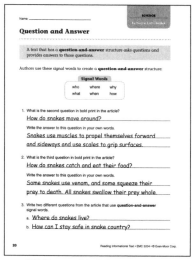

TE Page 20 / SB Page 12

Unit 2

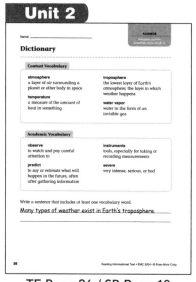

TE Page 26 / SB Page 18

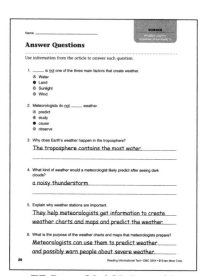

TE Page 28 / SB Page 20

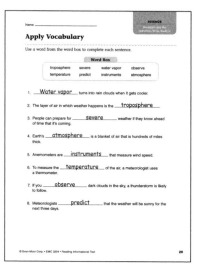

TE Page 29 / SB Page 21

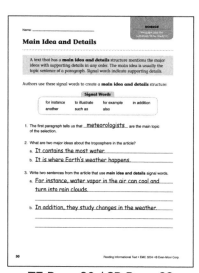

TE Page 30 / SB Page 22

Unit 3

TE Page 36 / SB Page 28

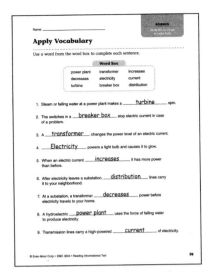

Answer Questions

Use information from the article to answer each question.

1. _____ is not a type of power plant.
   Ⓐ Nuclear
   Ⓑ Coal-fired
   ● Substation
   Ⓓ Hydroelectric

2. According to the article, a spinning turbine _____.
   Ⓐ increases the energy of falling water
   ● moves a coil of wire between magnets
   Ⓒ carries electricity to homes in your town
   Ⓓ stops the flow of electricity if there is a problem

3. What materials listed in the article can power plants use to create electricity?
   steam and falling water

4. What is the purpose of transmission lines?
   They carry electric currents over long distances.

5. Explain the purpose of a breaker box.
   It can stop an electric current if there is a problem.

6. According to the article, what is the complete loop made by an electric current?
   It goes from the power plant to a house and back to the power plant again.

TE Page 38 / SB Page 30

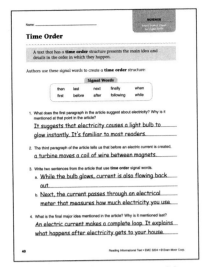

Apply Vocabulary

Use a word from the word box to complete each sentence.

Word Box

power plant	transformer	increases
decreases	electricity	current
turbine	breaker box	distribution

1. Steam or falling water at a power plant makes a __turbine__ spin.

2. The switches in a __breaker box__ stop electric current in case of a problem.

3. A __transformer__ changes the power level of an electric current.

4. __Electricity__ powers a light bulb and causes it to glow.

5. When an electric current __increases__, it has more power than before.

6. After electricity leaves a substation, __distribution__ lines carry it to your neighborhood.

7. At a substation, a transformer __decreases__ power before electricity travels to your home.

8. A hydroelectric __power plant__ uses the force of falling water to produce electricity.

9. Transmission lines carry a high-powered __current__ of electricity.

TE Page 39 / SB Page 31

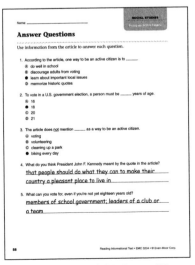

Time Order

A text that has a **time order** structure presents the main idea and details in the order in which they happen.

Authors use these signal words to create a **time order** structure:

Signal Words

| then | last | next | finally | when |
| first | before | after | following | while |

1. What does the first paragraph in the article suggest about electricity? Why is it mentioned at that point in the article?
   It suggests that electricity causes a light bulb to glow instantly. It's familiar to most readers.

2. The third paragraph of the article tells us that before an electric current is created, a turbine moves a coil of wire between magnets.

3. Write two sentences from the article that use **time order** signal words.
   a. While the bulb glows, current is also flowing back out.
   b. Next, the current passes through an electrical meter that measures how much electricity you use.

4. What is the final major idea mentioned in the article? Why is it mentioned last?
   An electric current makes a complete loop. It explains what happens after electricity gets to your house.

TE Page 40 / SB Page 32

Unit 4

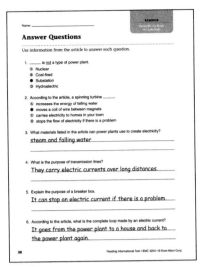

Dictionary

Content Vocabulary

continental drift
the slow movement of Earth's continents as tectonic plates shift

tectonic plates
huge sheets of rock that make up Earth's surface

mantle
a thick layer of rock beneath Earth's surface that, due to high heat, moves very slowly

Academic Vocabulary

coastline
the boundary between land and an ocean or lake

theory
an idea of how something works

surface
the outside or top of something; the part of land or water that touches the air above it

currents
streams of flowing air, matter, or energy that move in a certain direction

evidence
facts that show a theory or belief to be true or false

Write a sentence that includes at least one vocabulary word.
Mason believes the theory that the universe is expanding.

TE Page 46 / SB Page 38

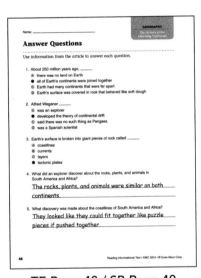

Answer Questions

Use information from the article to answer each question.

1. About 250 million years ago, _____.
   Ⓐ there was no land on Earth
   ● all of Earth's continents were joined together
   Ⓒ Earth had many continents that were far apart
   Ⓓ Earth's surface was covered in rock that behaved like soft dough

2. Alfred Wegener _____.
   Ⓐ was an explorer
   ● developed the theory of continental drift
   Ⓒ said there was no such thing as Pangaea
   Ⓓ was a Spanish scientist

3. Earth's surface is broken into giant pieces of rock called _____.
   Ⓐ coastlines
   Ⓑ currents
   Ⓒ layers
   ● tectonic plates

4. What did an explorer discover about the rocks, plants, and animals in South America and Africa?
   The rocks, plants, and animals were similar on both continents.

5. What discovery was made about the coastlines of South America and Africa?
   They looked like they could fit together like puzzle pieces if pushed together.

TE Page 48 / SB Page 40

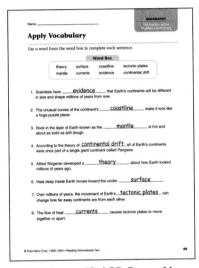

Apply Vocabulary

Use a word from the word box to complete each sentence.

Word Box

| theory | surface | coastline | tectonic plates |
| mantle | currents | evidence | continental drift |

1. Scientists have __evidence__ that Earth's continents will be different in size and shape millions of years from now.

2. The unusual curves of the continent's __coastline__ make it look like a huge puzzle piece.

3. Rock in the layer of Earth known as the __mantle__ is hot and about as solid as soft dough.

4. According to the theory of __continental drift__, all of Earth's continents were once part of a single giant continent called Pangaea.

5. Alfred Wegener developed a __theory__ about how Earth looked millions of years ago.

6. Heat deep inside Earth moves toward the cooler __surface__.

7. Over millions of years, the movement of Earth's __tectonic plates__ can change how far away continents are from each other.

8. The flow of heat __currents__ causes tectonic plates to move together or apart.

TE Page 49 / SB Page 41

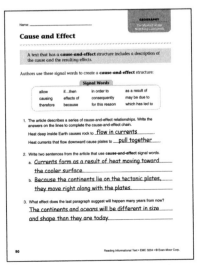

Cause and Effect

A text that has a **cause-and-effect** structure includes a description of the cause and the resulting effects.

Authors use these signal words to create a **cause-and-effect** structure:

Signal Words

allow	if...then	in order to	as a result of
causing	effects of	consequently	may be due to
therefore	because	for this reason	which has led to

1. The article describes a series of cause-and-effect relationships. Write the answers on the lines to complete the cause-and-effect chain.
   Heat deep inside Earth causes rock to __flow in currents__
   Heat currents that flow downward cause plates to __pull together__

2. Write two sentences from the article that use **cause-and-effect** signal words.
   a. Currents form as a result of heat moving toward the cooler surface.
   b. Because the continents lie on the tectonic plates, they move right along with them.

3. What effect does the last paragraph suggest will happen many years from now?
   The continents and oceans will be different in size and shape than they are today.

TE Page 50 / SB Page 42

Unit 5

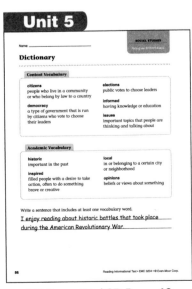

Dictionary

Content Vocabulary

citizens
people who live in a community or who belong by law to a country

democracy
a type of government that is run by citizens who vote to choose their leaders

elections
public votes to choose leaders

informed
having knowledge or education

issues
important topics that people are thinking and talking about

Academic Vocabulary

historic
important in the past

inspired
filled people with a desire to take action, often to do something brave or creative

local
in or belonging to a certain city or neighborhood

opinions
beliefs or views about something

Write a sentence that includes at least one vocabulary word.
I enjoy reading about historic battles that took place during the American Revolutionary War.

TE Page 56 / SB Page 48

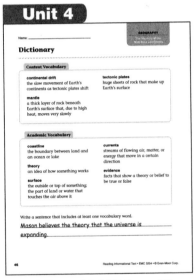

Answer Questions

Use information from the article to answer each question.

1. According to the article, one way to be an active citizen is to _____.
   Ⓐ do well in school
   Ⓑ discourage adults from voting
   ● learn about important local issues
   Ⓓ memorize historic quotes

2. To vote in a U.S. government election, a person must be _____ years of age.
   Ⓐ 16
   ● 18
   Ⓒ 20
   Ⓓ 21

3. The article does not mention _____ as a way to be an active citizen.
   Ⓐ voting
   Ⓑ volunteering
   Ⓒ cleaning up a park
   ● biking every day

4. What do you think President John F. Kennedy meant by the quote in the article?
   that people should do what they can to make their country a pleasant place to live in

5. What can you vote for, even if you're not yet eighteen years old?
   members of school government; leaders of a club or a team

TE Page 58 / SB Page 50

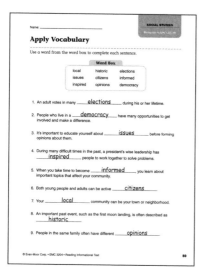

TE Page 59 / SB Page 51

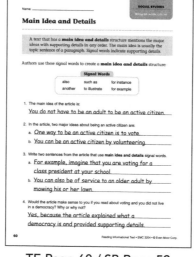

TE Page 60 / SB Page 52

TE Page 66 / SB Page 58

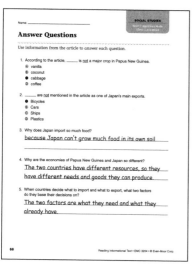

TE Page 68 / SB Page 60

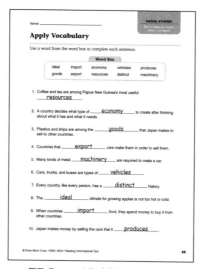

TE Page 69 / SB Page 61

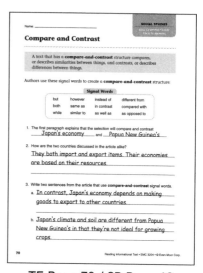

TE Page 70 / SB Page 62

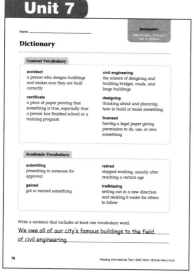

TE Page 76 / SB Page 68

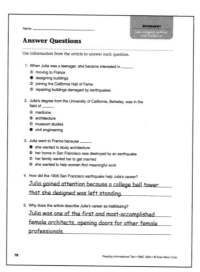

TE Page 78 / SB Page 70

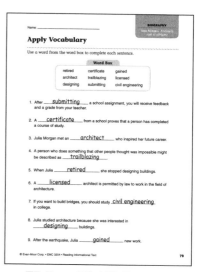

TE Page 79 / SB Page 71

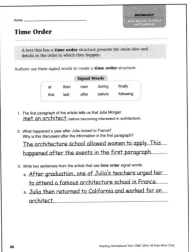

TE Page 80 / SB Page 72

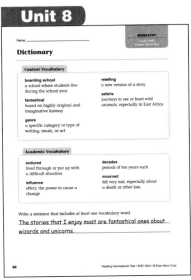

TE Page 86 / SB Page 78

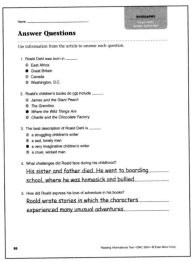

TE Page 88 / SB Page 80

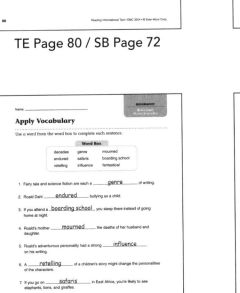

TE Page 89 / SB Page 81

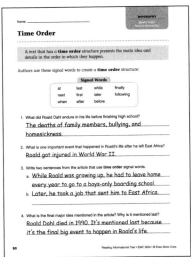

TE Page 90 / SB Page 82

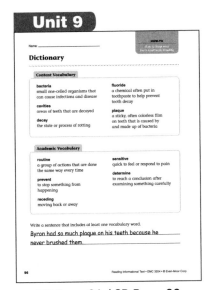

TE Page 96 / SB Page 88

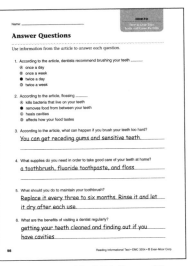

TE Page 98 / SB Page 90

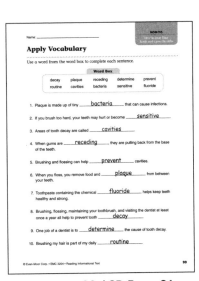

TE Page 99 / SB Page 91

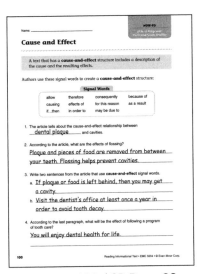

TE Page 100 / SB Page 92

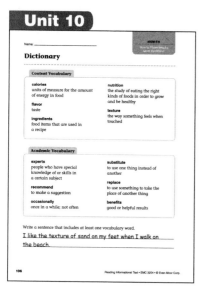

TE Page 106 / SB Page 98

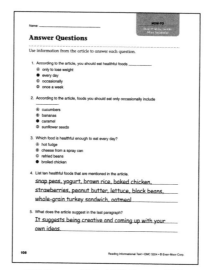

TE Page 108 / SB Page 100

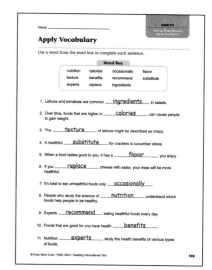

TE Page 109 / SB Page 101

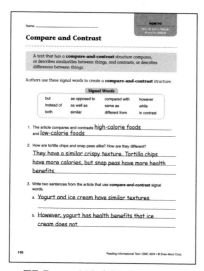

TE Page 110 / SB Page 102

Common Core Mastery

Text-Based Writing Nonfiction

Grade 4

SAMPLER

Animals Helping Humans

Lesson Objectives

Writing
Students use information from the social studies article to write a compare-and-contrast essay.

Vocabulary
Students learn content vocabulary words and use those words to write about how service animals are alike and different.

Content Knowledge
Students learn the wide variety of tasks that service animals perform for humans.

Essential Understanding
Students understand that people with disabilities can live regular lives with assistance from service animals.

Prepare the Unit

Reproduce and distribute one copy for each student.

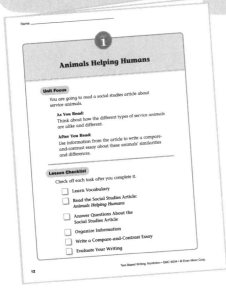

1 Unit Focus and Lesson Checklist

Distribute one unit to each student and direct students' attention to the Unit Focus and Lesson Checklist. Tell them they will be able to refer to the focus of the unit as needed while working on the lessons. Instruct students to check off each task on the checklist after they complete it.

Read aloud the focus statements, and verify that students understand their purpose for reading. Ask:

- *What are we going to read about?* (service animals)

- *What are you going to learn about them?* (how they are alike and different)

- *What are you going to write based on this article?* (a compare-and-contrast essay)

CCSS: **W** 4.2, 4.7, 4.8   **RIT** 4.3, 4.4, 4.5, 4.10

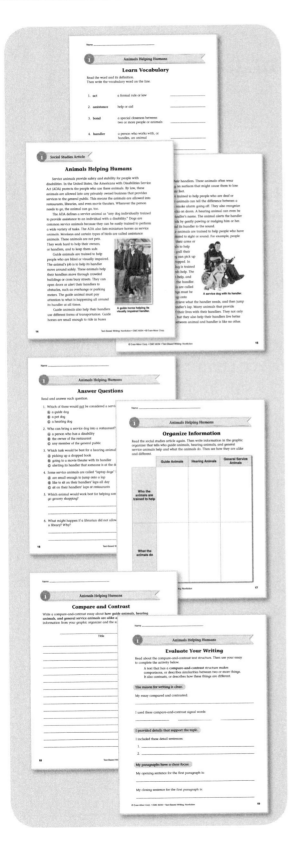

2 Learn Vocabulary

Read aloud each content vocabulary word and have students repeat. Then read aloud and discuss the definitions. Explain that students will have a better understanding of the words after they read the social studies article. Have students write the vocabulary words on the provided lines.

3 Read the Social Studies Article: *Animals Helping Humans*

Read aloud the social studies article as students follow along silently. Then have students reread the article independently or in small groups.

4 Answer Questions About the Social Studies Article

To ensure reading comprehension, have students answer the text-dependent questions. Review the answers together.

5 Organize Information

Explain to students that they will use a compare-and-contrast graphic organizer to help them plan their essays. Guide students in using the text to complete the organizer.

6 Write a Compare-and-Contrast Essay

Have students complete the writing assignment independently, with a partner, or in small groups.

Review the structure of a compare-and-contrast essay and the related signal words:

- Explains similarities and differences between two or more things

- Signal words: *same, alike, also, as well, both; different, however, but, while, instead of*

7 Evaluate Your Writing

Explain that students will evaluate their writing to ensure that they have produced well-written essays that follow the compare-and-contrast text structure.

Animals Helping Humans

Unit Focus

You are going to read a social studies article about service animals.

As You Read:

Think about how the different types of service animals are alike and different.

After You Read:

Use information from the article to write a compare-and-contrast essay about these animals' similarities and differences.

Lesson Checklist

Check off each task after you complete it.

- [ ] **Learn Vocabulary**
- [ ] **Read the Social Studies Article:** *Animals Helping Humans*
- [ ] **Answer Questions About the Social Studies Article**
- [ ] **Organize Information**
- [ ] **Write a Compare-and-Contrast Essay**
- [ ] **Evaluate Your Writing**

Learn Vocabulary

Read the word and its definition.
Then write the vocabulary word on the line.

1. **act**   a formal rule or law   _____

2. **assistance**   help or aid   _____

3. **bond**   a special closeness between
                    two or more people or animals   _____

4. **handler**   a person who works with, or
                    handles, an animal   _____

5. **impaired**   weakened or less able   _____

6. **obstacles**   things that are physically in
                    front of a person who is trying
                    to move   _____

7. **public**   all the people in an area   _____

8. **service**   helpful; working for another   _____

Animals Helping Humans

Service animals provide safety and stability for people with disabilities. In the United States, the Americans with Disabilities Service Act (ADA) protects the people who use these animals. By law, these animals are allowed into any privately owned business that provides services to the general public. This means the animals are allowed into restaurants, libraries, and even movie theaters. Wherever the person needs to go, the animal can go, too.

The ADA defines a service animal as "any dog individually trained to provide assistance to an individual with a disability." Dogs are common service animals because they can be easily trained to perform a wide variety of tasks. The ADA also lists miniature horses as service animals. Monkeys and certain types of birds are called assistance animals. These animals are not pets. They work hard to help their owners, or handlers, and to keep them safe.

Guide animals are trained to help people who are blind or visually impaired. The animal's job is to help its handler move around safely. These animals help their handlers move through crowded buildings or cross busy streets. They can open doors or alert their handlers to obstacles, such as overhangs or parking meters. The guide animal must pay attention to what is happening all around its handler at all times.

A guide horse helping its visually impaired handler.

Guide animals also help their handlers use different forms of transportation. Guide horses are small enough to ride in buses

Text-Based Writing: Nonfiction • EMC 6034 • © Evan-Moor Corp.

and in some cars with their handlers. These animals often wear special shoes for walking on surfaces that might cause them to lose their balance or hurt their feet.

Hearing animals are trained to help people who are deaf or hearing impaired. These animals can tell the difference between a telephone ringing and a smoke alarm going off. They also recognize emergency sirens or knocks on doors. A hearing animal can even be trained to listen for its handler's name. The animal alerts the handler when it hears these sounds by gently pawing or nudging him or her. Then the animal will lead its handler to the sound.

Other general service animals are trained to help people who have a disability that is not related to sight or sound. For example, people who cannot walk or use their arms or hands use service animals to help them walk steadily or to pull their wheelchair. A service dog can pick up things its handler has dropped. In public places, a service dog is trained to bark if its handler needs help. The dog will find someone to help, and then lead that person to the handler.

A service dog with its handler.

Some service animals are called "laptop dogs." Laptop dogs must be small and able to jump up onto counters. The dog will retrieve what the handler needs, and then jump with the item onto its handler's lap. Many animals that provide assistance spend most of their lives with their handlers. They not only provide companionship, but they also help their handlers live better lives. The special bond between animal and handler is like no other.

Name _____

Answer Questions

Read and answer each question.

1. Which of these would <u>not</u> be considered a service dog?

    Ⓐ a guide dog

    Ⓑ a pet dog

    Ⓒ a hearing dog

2. Who can bring a service dog into a restaurant?

    Ⓐ a person who has a disability

    Ⓑ the owner of the restaurant

    Ⓒ any member of the general public

3. Which task would be best for a hearing animal to perform?

    Ⓐ picking up a dropped book

    Ⓑ going to a movie theater with its handler

    Ⓒ alerting its handler that someone is at the door

4. Some service animals are called "laptop dogs" because they ____.

    Ⓐ are small enough to jump onto a lap

    Ⓑ like to sit on their handlers' laps all day

    Ⓒ sit on their handlers' laps at restaurants

5. Which animal would work best for helping someone in a wheelchair go grocery shopping?

    _____

    _____

6. What might happen if a librarian did not allow a service dog into a library? Why?

    _____

    _____

Name _____

Organize Information

Read the social studies article again. Then write information in the graphic organizer that tells who guide animals, hearing animals, and general service animals help and what the animals do. Then see how they are alike and different.

	Guide Animals	Hearing Animals	General Service Animals
Who the animals are trained to help			
What the animals do			

Compare and Contrast

Write a compare-and-contrast essay about **how guide animals, hearing animals, and general service animals are alike and different**. Use information from your graphic organizer and the social studies article.

_____
Title

_____

_____

_____

_____

_____

_____

_____

_____

_____

_____

_____

_____

_____

Evaluate Your Writing

Read about the compare-and-contrast text structure. Then use your essay to complete the activity below.

> A text that has a **compare-and-contrast** structure makes comparisons, or describes similarities between two or more things. It also contrasts, or describes how these things are different.

The reason for writing is clear.

My essay compared and contrasted:

_____

I used these compare-and-contrast signal words:

_____   _____   _____

I provided details that support the topic.

I included these detail sentences:

1. _____

2. _____

My paragraphs have a clear focus.

My opening sentence for the first paragraph is:

_____

My closing sentence for the first paragraph is:

_____